T·H·E N·E·W
RELIGIOUS
POLITICAL
R·I·G·H·T
☐IN AMERICA☐

SAMUEL S. HILL & DENNIS E. OWEN

Abingdon
Nashville

THE NEW RELIGIOUS/POLITICAL RIGHT IN AMERICA

Copyright © 1982 by Abingdon

All rights reserved.
No part of this book may be reproduced in any manner whatsoever without written permission of the publisher except brief quotations embodied in critical articles or reviews. For information address Abingdon, Nashville, Tennessee.

Library of Congress Cataloging in Publication Data

HILL, SAMUEL S.
    The new religious/political right in America.
    Includes bibliographical references.
    1. United States—Politics and government—1977–1981.
    2. United States—Politics and government—1981–
    3. Conservatism—United States—History—20th century.
    4. Christianity and politics. 5. Fundamentalism—History.
    6. Evangelicalism—United States—History—20th century.
    I. Owen, Dennis E. (Dennis Edward), 1944–. II. Title.
    E872.H54   261.7'0973   81-20661   AACR2

                    ISBN 0-687-27867-8

Scripture quotations noted RSV are from the Revised Standard Version of the Bible, copyrighted 1946, 1952, © 1971, 1973 by the Division of Christian Education of the National Council of the Churches of Christ in the U.S.A. and are used by permission. All others are from the King James Version.

MANUFACTURED BY THE PARTHENON PRESS AT
NASHVILLE, TENNESSEE, UNITED STATES OF AMERICA

We dedicate this book to

Two Scholars who have illuminated so much—
Robert N. Bellah
Martin E. Marty

A Local Pastor who sees so clearly the
relationship between Religion and America—
John Pearson

A Conservative Politician who lost to conservatives,
but who maintained integrity before, during, and after—
John Buchanan

BRIDWELL LIBRARY
SOUTHERN METHODIST UNIVERSITY
DALLAS, TEXAS 75275

CONTENTS

PREFACE

The timing of this book is unusually significant. Who had heard of a new religious/political conservative cause and crusade in America before 1979? Hardly anyone, largely because nothing of that kind of any size or influence existed in the public life of American society. It has come into existence recently and rapidly, and acquired a great deal of attention, both enthusiastic support and heated opposition.

In the campaigns leading up to the fall elections of 1980, the words Moral Majority burst into prominence. That term came to stand for a sizable and ever-so-dedicated segment of the population—conservative or even Fundamentalist in religion, and conservative in politics—which brought its concerns to focus on a specific list of issues. Concerning this New Religious/Political Right (NRPR), much confusion abounds, not to mention consternation. We, two professional students of religion as a force in culture, believing as we do that knowledge and understanding contribute to a civilized life, determined to attempt to clarify and interpret this phenomenon. We hope that the fruits of our decision will prove illuminating.

The analysis that follows is meant to be scrupulously fair. If any shrill tones emanate—at least any that are due to the authors' attitudes or manner of expression—we are regretful, because that is very far from our intention. Our aim has been to understand the NRPR on its own terms. But we have had to do so in a context, from a perspective, of course. And because the NRPR is a public force which affects the well-being of American society, we have, rather naturally, been obligated to do some assessing of its promise for the health and direction of that society.

The reader will see that we have reached the conclusion that its impact on our common life will be limited. A movement to be noted and taken seriously, yes. A movement that is likely to alter the basic course of American public life, probably not. Our assessment is largely negative—not harsh or condescending, but negative. It may be summarized in this way: The NRPR is neither biblical nor Constitutional enough to recommend itself as a constructive element. Rather than recalling us to a putative heritage and destiny, it threatens to divert us by creating a new course, one that does not do profound justice to our religion or to our politics, and in any event, is not edifying. We grant that the NRPR has diagnosed a number of our nation's ills with some acumen. But its supply of understanding is short, and its prescribed cure lacks power to heal.

Two quite different people, colleagues in the Department of Religion at the University of Florida, have collaborated to produce this study. We chose to divide the labor rather than write all the material jointly. The senior co-author (S.S.H.) would like to acknowledge, with respect and appreciation, that the larger share of the research and writing has been done by the younger co-author (D.E.O.).

Our gratitude is extended to a number of generous people. Staff members of Moral Majority, Inc., the Christian Broadcasting Network, and the National Religious Broadcasters come quickly to mind; similarly, many people associated with a variety of governmental and lobbying agencies in Washington, D.C. Two individuals deserve singling out: Ann H. Scudder of that city and of Gainesville, and L. Phillip Sheldon of Christian Voice. Not all our benefactors are far away, however: "Home folks" Austin B.

Creel, Marilyn K. Gallington, and Richard L. Harris really came
through for us.

   To those many we offer our thanks. And to all who examine this
book, we express our hope that such words as *fair, perceptive,
constructive,* and *informative* characterize its every page.

Samuel S. Hill
Dennis E. Owen
Gainesville, Florida
July 2, 1981

CHAPTER 1

The Phenomenon: The NRPR—What Is It?

Way back in 1976, a number of Americans were concerned about the candidacy and potential election of a born-again Christian from the Deep South. How quickly the tide turned! In 1980, forthright conservatism dominated the political mood nationwide, and the man elected President was linked, in complex and curious ways, with strident religious conservatism.

The election of Ronald Reagan resulted in part because some particular moral/spiritual attitudes were becoming prominent in the society. That fact is intriguing, since Reagan did not have a conspicuously religious reputation.

In one sense there was nothing very new or susprising about these developments. From the beginning, American political life has become accustomed to the fact that religion plays some part in who is nominated for public office and who is elected. The religious affiliation or orientation of a person who aspires to the county commission, or the state legislature, or the national Congress, or even to the Presidency, is a matter of public curiosity and interest. His or her support from the electorate, or more probably, from people with a certain religious style of outlook, irrespective of affiliation, may very well draw upon the candidate's membership in this or that denomination.

Political life has become *accustomed,* yes, but not habituated. Sometimes religion plays little or no part; sometimes it stands out as one of several major factors. If we take the office of President as an example, we can observe some correlation between a candidate's religious outlook or affiliation and his voter appeal. Alfred E. Smith's Roman Catholicism was a major campaign issue in the election of 1928; in quite different and much smaller ways—and with a signally different result!—the same may be said of the Catholicism of John F. Kennedy in 1960. Far more subtle and complex were the Presidential elections of 1976 and 1980.

A number of people were concerned that Jimmy Carter's Southern Baptist brand of Protestantism—born-again religion, it was called—would make him dangerous. Specifically, many wondered whether he would use the nation's highest office to impose his fervent faith on others. Or whether his religious (and regional) manner would render him unsophisticated and ineffective in dealing with cosmopolitan people and issues. Or, most troublesome of all, whether his piety and supernaturalism would not make him naïve and commit him to a simplistic moralism in a world of power politics. Looking back, we can see that while his faith did affect his stance and priorities, it was hardly a liability or menace to his conduct of the office. Certainly no one can argue successfully that Carter's religious perspective dominated his thinking on all topics, making him narrow-minded or provincial, or in any way a bigot.

The election of 1980 was, if anything, far more suffused with religious talk and concerns. That this should have been the case when Jimmy Carter was running against Ronald Reagan is amazing. Carter's born-again faith had become no issue at all. The religious discussions swirled around Reagan, hardly a person suitably described as born again, or pious, or fervent, or an Evangelical—certainly not a religious extremist or fanatic, indeed not a man very up-front about his personal faith. In fact, it is even more astonishing that Reagan's divorce from his first wife, even though it took place thirty years before, was simply not mentioned.

Yet Ronald Reagan, the not very pious or religiously demonstrative person, was the hero of a large segment of religiously conservative America—almost a Messianic figure. Many announced that they were pinning their hopes on him. He was spoken of as God's man for this hour in the national life. Who, we must ask, said and believed these things? And what was there about Reagan, and their perception of him, that wedded constituency and candidate?

Who, in this case, is the New Religious/Political Right in American society. Often lumped together and called the Moral Majority, which is, in fact, the name of one organization within this informal coalition, these groups are more accurately called the NRPR. What is their platform? High on the list of their causes is a fear of moral and spiritual deterioration of life in the United States of America. A great many of these people are from the Evangelical and Fundamentalist families of Protestantism. (These differ; we will give their respective profiles later.) A great many others seem to be political conservatives without strong religious commitments, but who stand in that huge throng of Americans subscribing to the special destiny of this land, to its need to remain faithful to its divine calling, and to a specifiable list of values. In 1980, certain prevalent practices were deemed to be at odds with such destiny, calling, and values.

Thus this phalanx of the pure in heart comprises devout conservative Protestants, together with some less religious fellow travelers who see eye to eye with them on the singled-out issues, sure that they have been called to be God's agents for rescuing America from its dash toward destruction. Typically, the greatest support comes from independent Baptist congregations. At this writing, not a single organized denomination has voted to endorse the NRPR—not even the "Fundamentalist sects" and certainly not mainline denominations. To be sure, some ultraconservative and dissident Methodists, Southern Baptists, and Roman Catholics lend their support; also some Mormons. But this is an independent-church phenomenon, by and large; perhaps its greatest outside support comes, as we have surmised, from the politically conservative people who would be members of such churches if they were members of any church. As to geographical distribution, all data gathered so far point to an area running from the South through the Midwest as the heartland of NRPR strength.

These are the folk who always have been politically conservative, who stand for a strong America both militarily and morally, who like local and detest central governmental power. These two regions have been our most homogeneous areas; in the Midwest, historically diverse ethnicity has melted into a vigorous Americanism. As for class stratification, the NRPR draws heavily from the ranks of the working class, that sector of people who are not long removed from economic and political marginality, but who now enjoy reasonable standards of living facilitated by jobs calling for skilled labor.

It helps also to see who does not belong to the NRPR. Many conservative Christians do not. One such group would be those descended from the left wing of the Reformation: the Mennonites, Amish, and Brethren, for example, where convictions run deep and identity is clear—most emphatically, the right of all others to live unmolested. Another group is composed of a curious medley of Roman Catholics, Southern Baptists, and Mormons who share certain outlooks with the NRPR, but whose vision is largely limited to and whose loyalties lie with their own communions; these, too, in odd and varied ways, practice a basic live-and-let-live policy. A third encompasses those conservative Protestants in sects and denominations alike who believe in minding the Church's own spiritual business and steering clear of involvement in worldly affairs. The final mention is of a cadre of Evangelicals who are, if anything, more active in the political arena than is the NRPR, but whose agenda is sharply differentiated: Instead of abortion, public schools, pornography, national defense, and homosexuality, they focus on war and peace, social justice, and radical Christian life-style.

The list of prominent conservative Protestant individuals and institutions declaring no affiliation with the NRPR is impressive: Billy Graham and Carl F. H. Henry; Wheaton and Calvin colleges; Fuller Theological Seminary; the Southern Baptist Convention. In disclaiming membership, Dr. Graham, the foremost evangelist of this century, has been quoted as saying: "I don't wish to be identified with them. . . . Morality goes beyond sex to human freedom and social justice. . . . Evangelists can't be closely identified with any particular party or person. . . . It would disturb me if there was a wedding between the religious fundamentalists and the political right."[1] Dr. Henry, the nation's most influential Evangelical theologian, is similarly skeptical and critical: "It does . . . reflect adversely upon Evangelicals when many show less interest in getting biblical truth and right into national life than in promoting a born-again candidate or in getting prayer back into the public schools. . . . To take the route of a Christian party is, in my view, a mistake."[2]

Such opposition, criticism, and disengagement does not faze the NRPR. It stands firm for its platform. In brief detail, the issues that forged this informal coalition on the Right were: (a) an opposition to governmental financial support for and general social tolerance of abortion; (b) a determination to restore the right of public schools to hold concerted moments of prayer on a voluntary basis; (c) a lament over the weakened military position of the United States over against the Soviet Union and a pledge to make this nation's military defense strongest; (d) hostility to pornography—actually, to any and all flagrant exhibitions of sex; (e) a commitment to defeat the Equal Rights Amendment and all forces that threaten to undermine the traditional roles of women in society. The fully extended list adds up to advocacy for strong families, a powerful nation, healthy public schools, and traditional gender roles. To the devoutly religious within the NRPR, the disease afflicting the nation is diagnosed as *secular humanism.*

Who practices this pseudofaith of secular humanism? The real enemies of the NRPR, the true secular humanists, are liberals: political, religious, and political/religious. The picture (often a caricature) drawn of these Americans is that they are people who take one or another of the following positions: (a) Every person is entitled to his or her own judgment about moral questions; (b) one should do whatever one wants, within responsible limits, of course; (c) all moral judgments are relative, or at least rooted in the particular situation; (d) the relation between absolute moral claims and each person's freedom and well-being is dialectical and tilts toward the latter. Especially in the case of (d), the secular humanist camp is heavily populated by "liberal" Christian people from mainline Protestant churches, including ministers and theologians.

The NRPR is a collection of world changers, visionaries dedicated to combating such enemies. They are Americans who pronounce judgment on the present drift of affairs. They live by a vision of what God wills for American society—which is a far cry from the way things are now! An aroused, purged, redeemed, and redirected America will be a refreshed America; it also will be a light to all the nations, Winthrop's "city on a hill" worthy of that lofty eminence, perhaps for the first time since Puritan New England.

The NRPR is called to apply all its might and main to building the perfect society—not the *good* society, but the *perfect* society, based on biblical righteousness and holiness. Fully realized, it would feature: (a) happy nuclear families; (b) clear sex roles; (c) family and church in charge of all important social processes; (d) government which exists to provide defense against enemies and to punish evil; and (e) the nation's recognition of the sovereignty of God. This utopian condition *can* be brought about (the optimism and confidence of the NRPR must be emphasized). It will come to pass through the formation of perfect faith: Godly action will flow naturally from a transformed interiority. Convert the individual; then elicit a total commitment from him or her, and each person will produce the moral fruits that characterize biblical holiness. These in turn will be expanded to the wider public realm, so that the laws and values of the society reflect those same moral/spiritual convictions. Regenerated individuals will produce a regenerate society. A regenerate American society then will be in a position to transform the global human community. But all this will occur only when Truth is honored—that is, when the values on this list are put into practice. It is self-evident that this is the Truth and that the Truth is rightly viewed only when it is seen in this way. Thus uniformity will result, but a uniformity derived from the fact that the nation has "come to its senses," meaning that its acknowledgment will be willing and free, not a result of compulsion or repression. The NRPR's confidence and aggressiveness stem from its epistemology, its certainty about the purity of what it knows—not, as one might be led to believe, from a raw thirst for the power to dominate.

We can point to some principles by which the NRPR lives, although it is unfair to imply that it is a homogeneous cluster of citizens—there is diversity and some disagreement. Those who fly the NRPR banner are apt to subscribe to most or all of these principles or positions: (a) American society is decadent and plummeting toward destruction; (b) while all have a legal right to a great diversity of position, some are clearly out of step with the divine intention and the American tradition; (c) the nation's health and survival are directly correlated with the morality of its public and private behavior; (d) positions are divisible into right and wrong, with the specificity of each clearly discernible if one's knowing antennae are correctly positioned; (e) the right way is obtained from divinely revealed authority in Scripture and the faithful interpretation of it; (f) wrong religious interpretations may be more harmful than the vision of some unreligious people; (g) the priority list of the crucial values may be, and has been, ascertained by a certain group of conservative Protestants; (h) those who are given the vision to see the right way are called to establish that version of righteousness as the law and practice of the land; (i) general culture is fallen and hence may not be trusted as a source of the *true* and *right;* (j) it is not dialogue and common search that divulge the Truth, but recognition of authority.

By sharp contrast, mainline religion is accused of living by several or all of the erroneous principles on the following list: (a) a sense of being at home in the culture; (b) the acceptance of responsibility for the culture at large and its entire population, which necessitates compromise, negotiation, and the weighing of priorities; (c) the affirmation of a philosophy of pluralism; (d) a quiet optimism that traditional religion will endure and that society will outlast insidious challenges to its continuance and health; (e) a comprehensive inventory of moral/spiritual concerns, with stress on the structural, and the classic ethical questions; (f) a belief that culture, too, is governed by the Lord of history, which results in a disposition to view cultural shifts as positive—or at least an attitude of "let's consider this new trend and see if it may not have some virtue"—for example, changing roles for women;

(g) a conviction that the most mature life for individuals and in society occurs in the give-and-take of alternative and even conflicting opinions and judgments; (h) a disinclination to divide the human race into the good and the bad, Christians and non-Christians, with an allied concern for the total good of all, rather than for the salvation of each and the defense of the Christian faith.

Having glimpsed the NRPR profile and some principles that distinguish "true" religion from "false," we may ask next about its character as a social movement, anticipating a fuller discussion later. In the context of American society, what is this movement? What animates it? How, in public terms, can we characterize it? Is it a hitherto extremist movement, gone public and central? Is it a counter-culture movement from the Right? Is it an ideologically conservative group, asking no more than equal time, its fair share, an opportunity to present its case? Is it dominantly a strong propatriotism movement, seeking an alternative to the public schools? Is it a sectarian movement which, paradoxically, uses the fruits of modern culture to put modern culture in its place? Is it a new Fundamentalism, lacking the firepower of the 1920s Fundamentalist movement that was informed by residues of nineteenth-century Evangelical Protestantism and some Reformed (Calvinist) intellectualism?

In other words, how should we classify the NRPR as a social movement? What is its makeup as a religious force within the context of American religious history and contemporary society? It is our aim in the pages of this book to follow some leads provided by these questions.

Chapter 7 will focus on Why now?—inquiring into the coincidence of this movement and these times. Here we can anticipate that treatment by asking, What has upset Jerry Falwell, Charles Stanley, James Robison, Jesse Helms, and the several million Americans who comprise the NRPR? What developments have brought matters to a head? What has prompted this cadre of concerned Christian citizens to mount such a vigorous crusade?

For one thing, things have gone about as far as they can go in the moral realm of the national life. Federal funds are used to pay for abortions. Television and movie screens openly flaunt suggestive sex. Gender roles have become badly confused, with unisex clothing and hair styles, overt homosexual identity, and mothers more devoted to their vocations than to their children and husbands. The public schools have been forced by government to abandon their traditional religious contributions to the society's health and direction through classroom prayer and Bible reading. Instead of approaching a rendezvous with destiny, this nation is careening off the precipice into moral degradation.

And government is responsible for much more in our decline. Its hand is in everything; its repression of rights and liberties victimizes millions every day. As objectionable as anything to the NRPR are government's misguided and futile efforts to be neutral on religious questions. The founding fathers never intended such, nor does the First Amendment to the Constitution call for a policy of abstention, neutrality. Thus whether by intrusion into people's lives or by distorting the Truth, government diverts American society from the course to which the Almighty Lord has called it and toward which the Constitution has directed it. In more localized and specific ways, both federal and state government have aroused NRPR ire by imposing excessive—and discriminatory—regulations on Christian schools, which have been established by these sectarians and separatists at an astounding rate within the past decade. No one believes this except the sponsors of these schools, but they believe it with a vengeance.

Closely related is another factor that has rallied the NRPR troops into battle—a battle we may call the symbol revolution. When the Supreme Court decision of 1963 outlawed concerted prayers in the classroom, a dark new day dawned in America. Others may argue that such activity was innocuous, bordering on inane, anyway; that praying an all-faith prayer and reading the Bible or reciting the Ten Commandments was hardly likely to nurture Christian or Jewish identity. But to the NRPR kinds of people, a sacred symbol had been attacked and discarded. Those few minutes rooted the consciousness and loyalties of the young in this God-ordained land. Their removal amounted to a spiritual betrayal, a denial of our special vocation. Negatively, it bespoke capitulation to the Devil through the establishment of the religion of secular humanism. The public schools, after all, have been one

of the two central institutions in American society held to be
virtually sacred. The NRPR correctly perceives their importance,
even if it cannot give the reason for it. By being instruments for
cementing a national identity and generating a social consensus,
public schools have played an indispensable role in the life of a
society that has no formal symbols of unification such as the
monarchies and established churches of European nations.

The ravages of secularization are seen to have progressed
dangerously far. The media—newspapers, and especially television
—have come to treat expressive Christians as exceptional, even
strange. A Fundamentalist or a born-again Christian is portrayed
as a weirdo, a person who, through not knowing any better, is an
embarrassment to us all. From the NRPR perspective, it is bad
enough that respectable Christianity hardly ever surfaces in the
media; it is worse that high-intensity religion is depicted as fit only
for the eccentric and fanatical. It is a high-priority item that music,
art, education, and science, which once were vessels for the
glorification of God, be rescued for that end from their present
burial place in the morass of principles which exalt man, attack
religion, and serve the Devil.

No wonder this legion of Americans has had a bellyful! No
wonder they have sounded the battle cry! Christian soldiers should
awaken from their pious retreat to do to death the forces of evil so
widespread and all-conquering in our land. In a manner of
speaking, the NRPR is committed to the restoration of
Christendom. The goal of its earnest prayers and energetic
endeavors is the building of a Christian nation, a godly society, the
kingdom of God on earth. Now, they know that any such
late-twentieth-century creation cannot restore the medieval
scene. Under those conditions, all (except outcasts like the Jews)
were Christians, all belonged to a single Christian institution, and
the Christian Supreme Pontiff was the equal or superior of the
monarchs of the various realms. Today diversity is too deeply
entrenched and the philosophy of pluralism too widespread for the
same degree of homogeneity to prevail—not to mention the force
of the American Constitution and the inevitable incursions of
nonbiblical religion into an America in constant interaction with
foreign peoples and philosophies.

The conversion of all to Christianity, or of all self-confessed Christians to conservative Protestantism, is not necessarily the goal envisaged. The NRPR plan is more modest and a bit different. It pictures a "democratic Christendom," or perhaps something more akin to the Christian theocracy that held sway in seventeenth-century Massachusetts, in which approximately 10 percent of the population held church membership (and thus was franchised). The Christian America, NRPR style, would feature some who are called to lead all to sanity and acceptable living. The strategy is to take over deliberately, under orders from the Lord, from those whom corrosion and weakness have infected with the pernicious philosophy of secular humanism.

For a great number of Americans, many religious people included, that would not be an attractive free America in which to live. For the people of the New Religious/Political Right, a nation so fashioned would be a refreshed Zion, a blossoming desert, heaven on earth, a society lovely beyond compare, because it would reflect the Lord's will.

CHAPTER 2

Where It Fits
Into the American Religious Tradition

The way politics and religion are related is an old American issue and a recurring question. The hallowed principle of separation of church and state, while always in need of interpretation and deepened understanding, is about as basic to American society as the Presidency, the right to vote, and freedom of the press. But that very fact highlights the need to explain what the principle means, what it permits and prohibits, how it came about, and its career in the history of this republic. We will be doing so throughout this book.

For one thing, it reminds us that their ways of belief and practice termed religious are important to the people who live here. No more now than they did in the 1780s do Americans assume that religion is a peripheral, passing, or suspect aspect of life in this society. The revolutionary actions of disestablishing religion, protecting diversity of expression, and (later in actual practice) acknowledging pluralism were vital and essential policies for the nascent nation. Those actions continue to be the law of the land, in letter and in spirit; and they remain vital and essential. Religion has a real importance for Americans.

We are convinced that no one intends even to challenge this constitutional correlation between church and state, much less to undermine it. That point must be established early in this study, or there will be much muddled thinking about the NRPR. It can be argued that this newly emergent company of several million Americans has fallen short of the spirit of the separation principle. But that is exactly right, it can be argued. Both ways, in other words. And no evidence exists that this large company has any gripe at all with the principle, the letter of the law. These people are aiming not only to make America better—to call it to its senses and restore it to its God-given destiny, as they put it—but they hope to reinforce, to make even stronger, the principle of separation of church and state. Whether their programs are really apt to do so is also a subject for consideration here.

Much of the argument of this book turns on the meaning of the separation principle, the NRPR's rendering of it, and the response, in turn, of many other millions of Americans to the NRPR position. We may postulate at the outset that, were the NRPR outlook to dominate life here, the result would alter mood and program, but not the Constitution. Its First Amendment stipulation that "Congress shall make no law providing for the establishment of religion" could and likely would remain intact.

Both the NRPR and its opponents—indeed, all Americans—thus line up within a classic American heritage, the importance of the interrelation of religion and politics. Our national policy derives principally from two sources. One source was establishmentarianism, the English pattern which issued in the public policy that state and church are allies in the building of a Christian civilization. That goal being humankind's highest achievement, both major agencies must collaborate in bringing it about. The second was religious individualism, the view that religion is a matter of personal experience and therefore something that lies beyond the scope of government or society to engender, nourish, or oversee. Calvinism helped bring both these theories into American society; its impulse in the second respect, most fully formed in Puritan, Presbyterian, Baptist, and Quaker breasts (in that order), was destined to become dominant.

The salient point is that the relation of religious institutions and personal religious experience to public policy and the health of society has been a critical concern from the beginning. How

strange that a society and state with no official religion should need
to deal with religion so often and so publicly. Or perhaps not so
strange; maybe what is really strange is that American society is so
religious, when it does not need to be. In this sense, the NRPR is
indeed acting in the best American tradition. It seizes the society's
historic commitment to religion and seeks to strengthen the liaison
between the two, lest either falter. Judging from the program it
actually promotes in campaign activities and by television, its
concern is greater for the society than for religion—at least for
religious institutions. It would reform the nation's ethical life by
bringing it into line with biblical (its version) and, it is asserted,
traditional American, morality. Yet many Americans who are
suspicious of NRPR goals, strategies, and policies judge that it
also wants to make Christians—Christians of a "Fundamentalist"
sort—of all Americans. Our impression is that while these zealous
people would like nothing better, they acknowledge its impossibil-
ity and, to the point being treated, the illegality of programs of that
kind. Thus at bedrock, they are concerned only to "clean up
America," and, accordingly, to honor the principle of separation
of church and state. But there is more to consider on that topic, as
we will see in chapter 8.

In the course of American history, a number of specific
strategies have characterized organized religion's response to the
religion/society issue. They are helpfully summarized in the title of
a book published in 1962, *From State Church to Pluralism.*[1] During
most of the colonial period, in most areas, one denomination was
officially recognized and subsidized: Congregationalism in the
North and Anglicanism in the South (the latter rather ineffec-
tually). However, before disestablishment, erosion was occurring
at the impetus of Presbyterians, Baptists, Quakers, and even
Roman Catholics and Jews. The fact of diversity was giving rise to
a philosophy of pluralism, which resulted in religious liberty and
the separation principle. For both demographic and political
reasons, democracy being in the air and soon in the law books, the
new society exchanged old European patterns for the bold policy
of "to each his or her own" in matters of religion.

That accomplished fact did not alter the actual practice greatly,
however. For the first half-century of the Republic's life,

Protestant Christianity remained the nation's religion. Practitioners of other faiths were marginal in a society designed as religiously homogeneous; sometimes they were persecuted for denying convention and being deviants. But an important change occurred: Now it was Protestant Christianity, not merely one denomination of that diffused tradition, that was in the saddle. However, it was only "in the saddle"—not the legally recognized church of the society. If Roman Catholics and Jews ever were to arrive in large numbers, this de facto condition would be challenged. And that is precisely what happened. The arrival of "hordes" of the former group in the years 1835 through 1850 and 1880 through 1924; and of the latter, in the 1840s and from 1880 until 1924, stirred up fears, antagonism, and some violence, but in the long run changed the face of the public role of religion in the United States of America. Diversity and a philosophy of pluralism preceded a practical commitment to the latter by decades; but its permeation of political, legal, and social institutions was occurring steadily, seeping little by little into the attitudes and values of ordinary citizens.

The various Protestant churches, from Methodist and Baptist on the Left to the more traditionalist Presbyterian and Episcopal persuasions, undertook to assume responsibility for public morality and the general health of the society. They addressed a wide range of issues: slavery, temperance, prison reform, public education, Sabbath practices, and so on. In those pre-Civil War years, distinctions between *mainline* and *evangelical, liberal* and *conservative,* were not sharply drawn; indeed, Protestant Christianity was regularly called *Evangelical* Christianity in that era. There is only one distinction worth making: The characterization just made applies to the North, while churches in the South moved briskly toward withdrawal from public concerns, except for the defense of slavery.

The relative unity of the Protestant program for society was smashed by developments in the 1880s. Two radically different parties emerged—the Public Party and the Private Party, they have been called—the two soon having nothing to do with each other.[2] The Publics condescended to the Privates as ignorant and obscurantist; the Privates dismissed the Publics as not even being

Christian. The Protestants who interpreted their calling as directing them to the "private" concerns of regenerate lives, pure congregations, and correct teachings were responding, in part at least, to the horrors of biological evolutionism, the corrupt character of life in the cities to which they were moving from rural America, all critical analyses of the biblical text, and the defacement of God's nation by Roman Catholic and Jewish ways. They turned their backs on such a changed and perverse society and turned inward on themselves, their singular righteousness, and their authenticity. In this period, a cluster of Christians rightly called Fundamentalists appeared for the first time. The earlier Evangelicals and these Fundamentalists were not the same classification of Christians. (Moreover the terms are not identical in the 1980s.) In *Fundamentalism and American Culture,* George M. Marsden traces the career of this movement and declares that it was "shaped by the American cultural experience." His compressed thesis runs as follows: "Fundamentalists experienced profound ambivalence toward the surrounding culture. . . . These American Christians underwent a remarkable transformation in their relationship to the culture. Respectable 'evangelicals' in the 1890s, by the 1920s they had become a laughingstock, ideological strangers in their own land."[3] It is not excessive to describe them as bitter, sour, withdrawn.

The direction and tone of the Public Party of Protestants were exactly opposite. They "got involved" in social concerns. They adapted to the contemporary—to current intellectual developments, current social conditions, and current organizational trends. Evolution, as a theory descriptive of biological and social change, was embraced and accommodated. Critical study of the biblical text was pursued with vigor and approval, thus revolutionizing theological education, sermons, and Sunday schools. The blights of poverty, crowdedness, low wages, and social discrimination were taken up as ministries to which Jesus was calling his followers—the social gospel. So much common cause persuaded the denominations to begin to relax their hold on specific traditions in favor of ecumenical Christianity—the council of churches movement. The more the Publics traveled in these directions, the farther they distanced themselves from the

Privates, to the minds of each. A collision course produced conflict and schism in the 1920s, but the paths called for no duplication of the routes traveled. Even commitment to one common goal, Prohibition, held jointly by all Fundamentalists and many mainline Protestants (the Public Party), could not generate any concerted activity, since they were so isolated from and antagonistic toward each other.

By the time of World War II, the contours of American religion presented a spectacle something like this: (a) mainline Protestantism, mainly in the North, tending to be "liberal" in theology and also in politics, at least in its denominational and clerical leadership; (b) Fundamentalism, also mainly in the North (a point to be noted!); (c) Evangelicalism of the Wheaton College variety, influential throughout the Midwest, "conservative," but less and less Fundamentalist because of its emphasis on personal piety rather than on doctrinal absolutism, and also because of its greater openness to culture; (d) Roman Catholicism, by now extensive, living largely to itself, spawning its own diversities, and its people finding increased acceptance in the society; (e) Judaism and Jews, similarly isolated, similarly achieving acceptance, but also surrendering some of its, and their, identity through accommodation and assimilation; (f) southern Protestantism, much more like the (northern) Private than the Public Party, but showing little similarity to Fundamentalism, having little interaction with Evangelicalism, and withal going its own separate way, bound up with regional customs, conventions, and traditions.

World War II began to confuse this sixfold classification. The Civil Rights legislation and its implementation in the 1960s pushed things a bit farther, as did "liberal" opposition to American involvement in the Vietnam war. Black people, operating often from a religious base, discovered and employed public power as never before, and the whole society was influenced by their efforts and accomplishments. Religion was reconfirmed in the experience of many black Americans; for many others, the new freedom facilitated a transition from traditional religiosity to a secularism of independent thinking and economic, social, and political ambition. Among white liberals there was a tendency to equate religion with ethics; for many, this meant a forsaking of church life and most theological convictions. The liberal mainline churches became more liberal. As arresting as were both of these developments, a third upstaged them in the late 1970s: Evangelicalism and Fundamentalism went public. Within both groups, a sizable minority began to concern itself with wider-ranging matters than defense of the faith and salvation of the lost. In one sense, they were actually rediscovering their heritage, especially in the case of those people properly called Evangelicals. Fundamentalists of certain sorts, many of whom were independent or marginally denominational, entered public life for the first time, emboldened to endeavor to harmonize the Kingdom with the Church. It is important to grasp the sharp distinction between these two socially involved groups of conservative Protestants. The intense, dignified, scholarly, middle-class company of Evangelicals are those associated with the "Chicago call" (of 1973 to social action), *Sojourners* magazine, and the Evangelicals for Social Action. The other group is a more demonstrative, aggressive, working-class collection of hitherto antisocial Fundamentalists. The two do not collaborate. Their stances and styles differ markedly. Yet they share (a) a history of disengagement from the public order, (b) a strong commitment to biblical authority, and (c) a fervent determination to realize God's will on earth. The NRPR attracts few if any from this group of Evangelicals; as for these Fundamentalists, they populate the movement to whatever (large) degree its clientele comes from confessedly Protestant Christian ranks.[4]

While precise data as to the profile of participants in the NRPR are not yet available, much suggestive evidence does present itself. We may be quite certain that the following organized communions contribute a small percentage of their members to the cause: the two large Presbyterian bodies (United Presbyterian Church in the U.S.A. [UPCUSA] and Presbyterian Church in the United States [PUCS]); the Protestant Episcopal Church; the three largest Lutheran bodies (Lutheran Church in America [LCA], American Lutheran Church [ALC], and Missouri Synod); the United Church of Christ; the American Baptist Churches; the Disciples of Christ; the Society of Friends (Quakers); the Eastern Orthodox bodies; and the several Mennonite and Brethren fellowships. Of the following denominations, larger percentages, but still a decided minority, do probably participate: United Methodist Church (more southern members than northern); Southern Baptist Convention; and Churches of Christ. The Protestantism of black America (there being seven large constituencies—three each of Baptist and Methodist, and the Pentecostal Church of God by Faith) is almost certainly represented by quite a number. While an observer may be in for some surprises once the facts come to light, one is inclined to hazard a guess that primary support comes from rank-and-file Fundamentalism, specifically: independent congregations—many Baptist, many nondenominational; the classical sects of American society—the Church of God organizations, the Assemblies of God, and the Pentecostal bodies. Officials of the NRPR report that Mormon involvement is substantial. It is the case that much of the moral platform of the NRPR fits Mormon values; however, most of its ways, styles, and approaches do not. Moreover, Mormon loyalties tend to be limited to "the church" itself. Even so, the support of individual Mormons and the consonance of NRPR morality with Mormon morality are facts worth noting.

The absence of gathered and refined data produces most pain at the point of the possible number of unchurched or very marginally churched people active in NRPR. In other words, what proportion of the movement is a political/religious commitment and not a religious/political concern? How many members candidly admit that they are not believers? More significantly, how many make use of religious symbols and rhetoric to bolster and legitimate moral/political positions held for other reasons? Of course one's religious and secular life are never purely separable, no matter which side takes precedence. But there is an important difference between the person with strong religious identification and commitments from which moral/political convictions emanate (as far as anyone can tell), and the person whose principal concerns are political/moral and who seems to append a religious foundation in order to reinforce his position. Here the quality of moralism may not be a respecter of types, and superpatriotism or social/political fanaticism possibly may arise from either quarter, but the individuals *are* different types of people.

To repeat the salient question: To what degree is the NRPR composed of people with weak religious commitment and identification, who gladly acknowledge alliance with a movement that is dedicated to high-intensity religion because a concern to reform America is a passion jointly held? We will begin to have answers soon, thanks to a cooperative effort of the National Council of Churches and much of the leadership of the electronic church, the major television ministries. This data gathering activity should be completed early in 1982. Many are heartened by this collaboration between two clusters of American Protestants who hitherto have had little to do with each other but who have volunteered to tackle this task jointly.

Summarizing, we note several central points: (a) The mainline Protestant denominations and the Roman Catholic Church provide few participants in the NRPR; (b) the "sect" denominations have not endorsed the movement; a minority of their members subscribe; (c) independent congregations, many of them Baptist, make up a large proportion of the following of the NRPR; (d) large numbers of the not-very-religious take the NRPR side and offer money and time; (e) Fundamentalists are heavily represented; (f) Evangelicals, as such, are not. In projecting such an analysis, we must underscore the difficulty of ascertaining the size, not only of the nonreligious following, but also of silent devotees in The United Methodist Church, the Southern Baptist Convention, and the Mormon community. A lot of people are "voting with their feet," although their institutional affiliation would seem to point them in other directions.

In this discussion we have sought to characterize the mentality and outlook of the NRPR and to place it in the setting of the American religious tradition. We may conclude by noting, first, that concern by organized religion for the health and direction of the society at large is as old as the settlement of North America. Only the party seeking to prescribe the health and set the direction is new. It is not composed of Christians in general or Protestants in general. The NRPR is certainly not composed of pluralists of goodwill, seeking to implement the Constitution. It is rather a company of American Protestants with some not-very-churched allies, who hitherto have been powerless, partly because they belonged to the working class and partly because their religion called them to repudiate entangling alliances with society. This group of right-wing Evangelicals has come into its own through ultramodern media—television and the computer—and now seeks to dislodge the liberal establishment in favor of a "traditionalist," "conservative," moral/spiritual consensus. If, for the past century, the moral tenor of American public life has been shaped by the leadership elite who have embraced a series of numerous new philosophies, allowing a kind of amorphous modernity to achieve consensus, the NRPR now yearns to establish a programmatic rectitude as the law and practice of the land. Dialogue should give way to authoritative standards, so that the nation can find its way back to sanity, to its destiny, and to God.

CHAPTER 3

Theological and Ethical Orientation

A great host of Americans are puzzled—in truth, confused and worried—by the Christian teachings on which the NRPR is based. Many want to know how its principles square with Christianity as generally understood.

Obviously the secular humanists don't know what to make of it, many of them incidentally being people of goodwill and high moral character, by classical ethical standards. Hardly any less perplexed by the NRPR's avalanche of preachments and activities are many millions of American Christians, of whom thirty or more percent are conservative, by traditional Christian standards. The response of Jews and their role in all this is a special case—Jews seem always to be a special case in a Christian civilization, as we shall point out in ad hoc passages elsewhere.

Conventional wisdom assumes that Christianity is all about love, God's creative goodwill toward all people, and their responsibility to return the favor by worshiping God and holding all other people in the same high regard that God does. More pointedly, God came to earth in the person of Jesus of Nazareth to incarnate that love, to create a community of followers (the Church), and to unleash the power of that enacted love toward the goal of a society permeated by compassion, justice, integrity, and altruism. In Christian theology, understanding and interpretation go farther and run deeper as they become particularistic. But on its public face, Christianity, for most people, is all about the description just given, or something like it—and they are correct. In the modern American setting, at least one other trait must be added: human free will—the right to interpret for oneself, the necessity of choosing religious faith for oneself—convictions which, for the great majority, imply the obligation to acknowledge all others' right to practice religion as they wish.

Where in this structure of belief does the NRPR fit? Probably the leaders of the movement would find little in the preceding statement to dispute, and not too much to quibble about. They would, of course, demur about stopping so soon. This is the point. The NRPR lacks the sense of levity, humor, distance from itself, and public responsibility necessary to divide the Christian structure of belief into two stages: the general, or public; and the particularistic, for insiders. In the name of creating a Christian public order, it denies the validity of Christianity's public face within a society that is more than diverse, in that it is legally committed to a philosophy of pluralism (roughly, *live and let live*). But the NRPR *is* making a contribution to our national life these days by forcing us to think about whether the First Amendment calls for the government to be religiously neutral, and whether secular humanism is a quasi religion which has acquired virtual "establishment" status.

But our national health is not enhanced by confusing the fundamental pluralism issue with the claim that making the public life of this society Christian is an acceptable goal.

How does NRPR theology arrive at its conclusions about what God wills and about what God is calling his saving remnant (in America, the NRPR) to accomplish? Its route should be perceptible to the great majority of Christians—up to a point, anyway—because it is parallel to routes traveled by Roman Catholics, Lutherans, Presbyterians, Methodists, Baptists, Pentecostals, and the rest. *Up to a point* is accurate, but that point is a rather advanced station along the way. The basic terms and concepts in the general Christian lexicon are familiar and treasured ones for NRPR Christians as well: God, Trinity, Christ,

Holy Spirit, Bible, sin, salvation, Church, redemption, love, responsibility, calling, purity, and so on. But the mix is different, the configuration distinctive. After the *point* is reached, the NRPR path diverges. And because the divergent path is built on the bed of the common ground, it is essential to note, also, that *common ground* is understood in significantly different terms. For example, *Christ, Bible,* and *responsibility* form a complex entity in the NRPR context which departs markedly from the shape it takes and the impact it makes upon other Christian movements, including most other Fundamentalist groups. As with everything else, in Christian theology the whole is greater than and different from the sum of the parts.

The NRPR theology shares with the general Evangelical community the twin commitment to what Marsden calls "complete confidence in the Bible" and a preoccupation with the "message of God's salvation of sinners through the death of Jesus Christ."[1] It also manifests the Evangelical temperament: intensity, certainty, aggressiveness, personal answerability, and similar characteristics. As such, it relegates to secondary or an even more remote position a great many other historic Christian teachings: the physical universe as divine creation, the providential ordering of all events, the Lord's Supper, the Incarnation, the Church, Christian education, ministries other than evangelism to non-Christian people, and the reluctance to claim that earth can know so much about heaven. Also missing are these styles of temperament: patience, taking the long view, listening to others, self-judgment, quiet confidence, a sense of humor and modesty about its own importance, and the like. Many have been accusing the NRPR of arrogant and imperious behavior. While that charge is defensible, it fails to get to the heart of NRPR intention and, presumably, its spring of action. Its intention, rooted in its theology, obliterates any boundaries between what it receives as divine revelation and what anyone else may perceive as true, whether attributable directly, indirectly, or not at all to divine origin. It knows what is best for all, because it knows the Truth. Thus, should the NRPR have its way, American society will be governed by laws that many would find distasteful, objectionable, and oppressive, not to mention contrary to the spirit of the Constitution and the Declaration of Independence.

What we have referred to as *obliterating boundaries* and, earlier, *not dividing into stages,* strikes at the heart of NRPR ideology. That philosophy wants to do everything, do it at once, and do it without consideration for what anyone else may think, hold dear, or be committed to. Skittish as we are about using the term, this philosophy bears some marks of *totalitarianism.* The gravity of the specter of some who tightly determine the moral and political life of all is offset by, we think, some decisive factors. In other words, we do not predict any such take-over, and we suspect that many in the NRPR may finally recognize that they are envisioning an ideal, as distinct from forecasting a fully realized kingdom of God. One factor is the program—rather limited, basically, despite the fears of the opposition—sponsored by the NRPR. If its announced plans (at present, at any rate) were all to become the law and values of the society, the following aspects of American life would go on, relatively unaffected: the basic structure and curriculum of the public schools; the manufacture and sale of alcoholic beverages; governmental subsidy of numerous amenities, facilities, and programs; the fundamental legal and political processes of the nation; a free press; public forums of all sorts; America's heavy involvement in the international community; periodic elections; and much more. A second factor, which supports the first, consists of those two sturdy documents which issued from the nation's natal decades. A third is the inevitability of shifting opinions and some public backlash to the increasingly brash and extremist strategies employed generally by the Right, with which the NRPR is heavily identified in the public mind (see final chapter).

The mention of a fourth factor brings us directly back to ideology—actually, theology and ethics. The NRPR wants its moral/political/economic views to dominate American life; it gladly supports candidates for office who are not its religious kinsmen but who take the right stands, and it will lobby and organize to achieve its ends. This indiscriminate support of individuals and groups could prove its undoing; at least, one suspects that a strongly held and shared religious basis would go farther toward solidifying its cause.

That the NRPR welcomes as colleagues many who are not serious self-confessed and practicing Christians certainly brands it as a novel form of Fundamentalism—or even of Evangelicalism. Classic Fundamentalists have had no more to do with godless individuals than with godless societies. Standard Evangelicalism has aggressively sought to win converts. History seems to teach us that having it both ways is difficult: Typically, one either minds the church's business on its terms and grows and consolidates gains, or one devotes energy to the implementing of God's will in addressing society's needs (and perhaps in cultivating a radical personal life-style) and runs some institutional risks in the process. Billy Graham and his fellow mass-evangelists have learned that lesson long since and have opted for winning converts. In the fall of 1980, Pat Robertson of the "700 Club" decided to withdraw from political activity in favor of spiritual ministries. To cite a different instance, the Evangelicals for Social Action and the Inter-Varsity Christian Fellowship usually hit the targets they aim at—serious study, intense discipleship, and involvement in others' lives. Having it both ways truly is difficult, and the attempt to do so may prove counterproductive. Perhaps Bill Bright and the Campus Crusade for Christ follow a more promising course than do Jerry Falwell and Moral Majority, in that they display Christian identity even when lobbying; they are more reluctant to make common cause with not-very-religious allies. The heart of the NRPR movement is preoccupied with attaining its political goals and gladly accepts support from people who are like-minded in public matters but not fervent practitioners of true-blue religion. Motivation and model emanate from the NRPR's conservative Protestant theology, but the religious credentials of its supporters are not checked at the entrances of voting booths or legislative halls.

To some readers it may seem that explicit theology is less vital a force than we have been led to expect of these "Fundamentalists." There are some surprises and peculiar twists, but a Christian understanding of things always lurks not far away. We are dealing here with the issue of authority; this is Christianity of an

authoritative—and often authoritarian—sort. The series begins
with acknowledgment of the Bible as the sole basis for all truth. It
extends to the functionally unchallengeable authority of Falwell,
the major interpreter, and other Fundamentalist leaders (as
chapter 5 argues). It concludes with a passionate devotion to the
accomplishment of the divinely ordained mission—in this case,
making a righteous America. But underlying all this is a principle,
which is also a metaphysical assumption, and a particular
epistemic usage: the principle of authority. The shape of God's
will has been revealed in Scripture. God's spirit gives precise
definition to the meaning of this message for America, through
guiding the minds and hearts of God's anointed leaders. By its own
lights, the NRPR is not hardheaded, stubborn, dogmatic,
imperious, or deaf to the convictions of others. On the contrary, it
is responsive to an unfailingly clear message from above. It is
convinced that others will be won over to the Truth as the Spirit
makes use of earthen vessels—Falwell, Robison, Stanley, Helms,
and their political organizations. Still others, the holdouts, the
intransigent, could hear this univocal message if only they would
listen.

The shape of this kind of thinking is an "ethic of the *right*" rather
than an "ethic of the *good.*" This is a *prescriptive* manner of
interpreting suitable behavior; what is written *(script)* comes first
(pre), before anything else. This approach does not accredit
questions such as: What is good for me, you, us? What do I want,
need, think is best? Rather, it asks: What is the great law? What is
True? Then an ethic of the *right* proceeds to deal with the crucial
question, What is required of me and us? Whereas *good* is
concerned with aspiration, hopes, goals, *right* speaks only of duty,
obligation, obedience to authority. Nor is there any sense of
ambiguity or dialetic, between Scylla and Charybdis, in the NRPR
position. The notion that what is *good* may have some bearing on
what is *right,* a standard mainline position, never occurs to such a
mentality.

It should be apparent that both ethical theories are strong and
that they have had lengthy careers in the history of Christianity.
No less apparent is the tenacity of an ethic of the *right* on the minds
of many in historic Protestantism—for example, many Calvinists,

most Evangelicals, and all Fundamentalists. What distinguishes
the NRPR within this substantial company is its "going public"
with these kinds of ethical convictions. It really does assert that it
knows what is *right* for all (not *best,* which is, after all, the
superlative of *good*) in a massive society built on democratic
principles based in a Constitution which has been interpreted
through a philosophy of pluralism for nearly two hundred years.

It is indeed strikingly ironic that the NRPR holds to a moral
philosophy so foreign to the American democratic tradition while
it is claiming to be the unique divinely anointed agency for the very
salvation of America. We are compelled to cry out, What a pity
that our judgment, which surely is shared by a host of fellow
citizens, cannot be heard for what it is: a plea to go back to the
primal sources, Bible and Constitution, for another look—this
time, with sensitive ears and hearts. The flaw in the NRPR
position is that it is not biblical or Constitutional *enough*. In
practice, this means the rejection of all postures of negotiation.
Negotiability does not characterize either the issues or the people
within the New Religious/Political Right. Moral judgments are
handed down, not arrived at in a forum. Political decisions are
declared, not concluded from the give-and-take of people who
respect one another's citizenship and engage in civilized dialogue.
Compromise, the very stuff of which public democracies are
made, is anathema—because it temporizes; it exalts the "traditions of men"; it trusts a process, rather than the Bible understood
as program.

It is precisely the nonnegotiability of the NRPR stance that
concerns other Americans. Almost everybody is perfectly happy
to let Fundamentalist Christians believe and practice their religion
as they choose. They are even willing to allow people of such
convictions to do battle for their causes in the public domain and
promote their candidates for office. What offends—and often
outrages—is the escalation of any group's views to exclusive
correctness, a blatant deafness to others' views, a blindness to the
fact that the God of the American experience wills both liberty and
law, both right and good, both conviction and quest. That God,
from biblical times to our own, runs risks—takes the chance that
purposive righteousness will not be deterred by the foibles of

humans, preferring that we stumble toward the goal rather than run a race rigged from the starter's gun. In one sense, the flaw in the NRPR outlook is its lack of trust in the Almighty Lord of the Hebrews, the Americans, and the whole world.

How earnestly we wish that Reinhold Niebuhr were in our midst for such a time as this. That great Protestant theologian (died 1971) would have directed unforgettably prophetic words against the NRPR (as he did against Nazism, communism, liberal utopianism, our thirty-seventh President, and all other arrogances of power—left, right, and center). Perhaps his brief essay on the "orders of creation" in the thought of Emil Brunner (died 1966) is as pertinent a treatment as any.[2]

Niebuhr concurred with Brunner that the family, economics, and the state are orders of creation—that is, that those arenas of life are not human constructions or historical accidents, but structures for living ordained by the Creator. Some such philosophy also pervades NRPR thinking. The issue is the way these orders are fashioned in the direction of God's will for all. In particular, how do societies avoid both anarchy and tyranny? Granted, the lack of rules, standards, and principles is intolerable and wrong. Also granted, domination, imperiousness, and totalitarianism are intolerable and wrong. Surely the God of love wills neither anarchy nor tyranny.

Niebuhr faults Brunner and the major Reformation tradition for fearing anarchy so much that it was betrayed by an attitude of "complacency toward tyranny." Continuing, he writes in the same vein: "The Reformation theory . . . gives the state the negative function of preventing anarchy" and in the process is "too complacent toward the peril of injustice and tyranny." Niebuhr then expresses his own normative judgment: "It would be better to regard anarchy and tyranny as the Scylla and Charybdis between which mankind must steer toward justice, fearing the one evil as much as the other."[3]

Precisely. Both (a) anarchy—relativism, lack of standards, each doing what is right in his own eyes, rampant egoism—and (b) tyranny—any one group, whether secular humanism or the NRPR, determining unilaterally what is right for all—must be held in check. And in everything, creative goodwill must prevail. In interpersonal terms, that means *love*. In an institutional setting, it means *justice* (which Niebuhr defines as *love distributed*).

The NRPR errs on the side of *tyranny*. And tyranny in the name of God is still tyranny. (Many historical instances come to mind.) Its end is not justice, but rectitude (of which domination is a predictable by-product). It does not finally take orders of creation seriously, since it is compelled to Christianize the whole public order, irrespective of dissenting convictions. It has nothing to say to non-Christians or to other varieties of Christians; rather, it works to frame the public context of their lives. It certainly has nothing to learn from them and no obligation to be concerned about their convictions and needs.

Thus, with assistance from Reinhold Niebuhr, we see the NRPR swapping one tyranny for another, laboring feverishly to rout the forces of the sovereign philosophy of secular humanism, which it is determined to replace with another sovereign philosophy—its own. We have here an authoritarianism run riot, a passion for courage and conviction gone to seed. If only the Americans who comprise the NRPR could be content to voice their positions and elect their candidates without a concomitant spirit of intolerance and domination!

An analogy drawn from Niebuhr's discussion of monogamous marriage is pertinent here. In treating monogamy as the highest form of the family, as an order of creation, he speaks of the mergence of two lives as being not a "fact of nature," but an "achievement of history." A genuine marriage partnership does not just happen, is not merely a legal estate. On the contrary, it is a relationship nourished and renourished, constantly and repeatedly, by two people who earnestly endeavor to blend commitment and warmth of relationship. Moreover, according to Niebuhr, any such mergence is "tolerable"—no more than tolerable—"only when grace sustains the partnership."[4] So it is also in the building of a wholesome public order such as we Americans would like to have. The events of 1776, 1783, and 1787 did not a United States of America make, nor do its ongoing institutional structures, symbols, and leadership. A wholesome society is an "achievement of history." Furthermore, only when "grace"—in public terms, *freedom, justice, rule of law, due process*—is present can the partnership involving 226 million fellow citizens flower and flourish.

To recapitulate: The NRPR lives with the burning conviction that the chaos, disorder, and deformity of recent and current American society must be set right. Anarchy, which comes in many forms, both overt and insidious—most undergirded by the philosophy of secular humanism—must be dispelled in favor of the triumphant rule of the divine law. The NRPR does not envisage the righteous society as resulting from a dynamic interaction between bipolar good, order, and justice, but puts all its marbles in the basket of order.

After a half-century and more of liberal domination, America has arrived at a sorry state. Should things continue on that course, disaster awaits. God would have no choice but to destroy any nation to which he had given so much and which had become so profligate. Destruction might come about gradually through internal disintegration, or it might result from the sudden appearance, the physical return, of the Lord Jesus Christ. Although NRPR theology does not dwell on the Second Coming, it most surely affirms it; it urges far and wide that people get their houses in order for the imminent return of the Lord. In fact, the theological setting for this concern that we be ready for that blessed eventuality is the divine call for the anointed ones to pronounce judgment on a nation that has abandoned its sanity and lost its way.

Those familiar with premillennial theology and with the NRPR's hard-hitting denunciation of sin might go on to suppose that there is little that can be done. Can any situation so dire be redeemed? But with an optimism that rivals in magnitude its assessment of the sordid depths to which America has sunk, the NRPR issues urgent pleas for God's people to get busy, in a spirit of ebullient confidence that this country can be turned around. Disaster can be averted! The message shouted from the housetops is that God will heal our land—and soon, if we will submit to his leading, in the moral/spiritual depths of our national life. This is apocalyptic thinking: A new day is dawning, a new world is coming! This is eschatological thinking: The End-time is coming!

Only the Lord can straighten out the mess, but Christians must do their part to bring about the new age of history. Grim assessment and buoyant confidence blend in the NRPR interpretation.

Much more could be said about NRPR theology and ethics by referring to its stand on the historic doctrines and teachings of Christianity. But more is to be gained by taking the next leaf straight from its own notebook. The distinctive position of the NRPR is, after all, practical—the embodying of the Lord's will in the way Americans live. Accordingly, we choose to include in this treatment a section on the major point at which "the water hits the wheel" for this group of American Christians. What is the NRPR's theological/ethical interpretation of the First Amendment to the Constitution? We are edified by examining the way it treats the hallowed principle of religious liberty, the policy often described as separation of church and state.

The NRPR vocally affirms the separation of church and state. One of its intriguing arguments is that this principle has been violated at a number of points. It believes that the state has been aggressively and oppressively hostile to the freedom of religion. It argues that the state has injected itself and its alien value-system into levels of the society where it has no right to be. For example, the NRPR has felt it necessary to argue that children do not belong to the state, but first to God, who entrusts them primarily to the care of parents and church. Education is perhaps the focal point of the NRPR's sense of violation, for it is in the public schools that it sees its children stealthily converted to a rival religion, secular humanism. The state is thus held guilty of having transgressed both the establishment clause ("Congress shall make no law respecting the establishment of religion . . .") and the free-exercise clause (". . . nor limit the free exercise thereof") of the First Amendment.

However, at the same time the NRPR affirms the separation of church and state, it calls for national repentance—not just of the individuals who comprise the nation, but of the nation as a collective entity. It is argued that America stands in the same relationship to God as did ancient Israel and, consequently, that America must acknowledge God's sovereignty and obey, or suffer the terror of God's wrath. The following excerpt from *Moral Majority Report* is a fairly typical expression of the NRPR position:

It is time to reject the godless, Communistic definition of separation of church and state that says there is no place for biblical moral law in public policy. We must honor the God who rules over the nations and said, "Whether therefore ye eat or drink or whatsoever you do, do all to the glory of God." Let us never forget that "the wicked shall be turned into hell, and all the nations that forget God."[5]

We are thus presented with rather contradictory tendencies: a sincere respect for separation of church and state on the one hand, and a thoroughly religious and sectarian view of the nation on the other. This tension exists within NRPR ideology primarily because it does not see its demand that the nation honor God and God's Word as a violation of the nonestablishment clause.

Vitually every NRPR tract that has broached the separation issue has begun by arguing that the separation of church and state does not mean the separation of God and government. The separation clause is interpreted as prohibiting only the establishment of a particular denominational state church. It is pointed out that numerous states retained established churches long after the adoption of the Constitution, although the NRPR's position today would be against such an arrangement. This point is brought forward to illustrate that America has a tradition not only of close alliance between church and state, but also of a thorough infusion of the state with Christianity. The presence of prayer in governmental bodies, pious statements attributed to our founding fathers, and religious inscriptions on buildings are generally marshaled as support for the NRPR's view. Essentially, what it seems to hope to demonstrate through these kinds of arguments is that America always has been a religious society; certainly, that separation of church and state has not meant in the past what it means today; and finally, that the arrangements of the past which allowed for a more explicitly Christian public order need to be reintroduced so that they will once again be normative.

In distinguishing church/state from God/government, the NRPR is arguing that the Constitution ought to be interpreted as allowing a kind of establishment of "religion in general." The idea is not a new one. *Harpers* magazine in 1858, for example, proclaimed that the separation of church and state did not mean that we should not have a national religion.[6] The NRPR view is essentially the same, except that the national religion it publicly espouses is not explicitly Christianity, as it was in the *Harpers* example. The NRPR would like America as a nation to acknowledge the biblical God and the authority of God's Word *without* establishing a particular religion. Martha Rountree, president of the Leadership Foundation, a pro-school prayer educational and lobbying group, made this point in her testimony before the judiciary subcommittee on the proposed school-prayer legislation: "We are not talking about religion. Religion is a doctrine or a denomination. We are talking about Almighty God, Creator of the Universe, of everyone regardless of denomination . . . or belief."[7]

Pointedly, the NRPR would like to deal with God and the Bible as if they were not matters of religion, but givens in the prereligious state of things. The Bible, for example, is treated as if it transcends religion. If we take religion in the Barthian sense of the human attempt to reach God, then for the NRPR, the Bible represents God's attempt to reach out to all of us. As such, the Bible surpasses religion and hence is exempt from any restrictions a society might place upon the exercise of religion. Consequently, the NRPR's call for biblical obedience is not seen as a violation of church/state separation, but a recovery of the proper relationship between church and state.

The NRPR is certain that it is correctly articulating God's will on a large number of specific moral, economic, and political questions. Furthermore, it is convinced that the activities of the state (and hence in the whole nation) will be judged by God according to biblical—largely Old Testament—standards and will be rewarded or punished accordingly. Thus religion is thought to bear the responsibility for saving the state. Simultaneously, the NRPR would like the state to impose biblical order and morality upon the nation in order to insure the survival of America and American Christianity.

The NRPR understands the state as a divinely ordained instrument for the preservation of order. Like the culture around it, the NRPR is deeply distrustful of the state in some areas, and yet trusting and optimistic in others. The particular areas of trust and distrust have been reversed, however. It is the view of the

NRPR that the state's primary task is that of defense—defense of the nation from external enemies, particularly communists, and defense of its people from internal antisocial behavior. In a sense, the police function of the state has become dominant, replacing the liberal and social-gospel view of the state as an agent of social change. The state's role is almost entirely negative—punishment is its essential activity. Jerry Falwell argues that the state is responsible for punishing evildoers, both domestic and foreign, and that it has a special responsibility to punish "the enemies of God."[8] (Dividing the world as it does into the forces of good versus the forces of evil, the NRPR assumes that atheistic communism is clearly God's enemy and therefore often calls for victory over it.) The state thus is God's terrible swift sword, not God's instrument for feeding the hungry or even for educating the population. These latter endeavors are seen ultimately as a demonic violation of God's established order, tending inexorably toward socialism, communism, and atheism.

The question of the state's relationship to those it governs is answered in a number of ways, occasionally in somewhat contradictory fashion. One of the more significant breaks the NRPR has made with the American Mythos is its rejection of what has been called the democratic faith. Its literature frequently makes the point that the United States is not a democracy, but a republic. The difference is held to be crucial. *Democracy*, for the NRPR, means *majority rule*, but with intimations of tyranny. In a democracy, so the concern is expressed, the majority is free to impose anything at all upon the entire society. Democracies thus allow for no minority rights. They also seem to tend toward the lowest common denominator. They are subject to whim; whatever suits the majority, no matter how perverse, becomes the law of the land. Furthermore, democracies, by locating sovereignty exclusively in "the people," tend toward the view that human beings are autonomous and hence subject to no higher authority than the collective appetite.

In contrast, the NRPR asserts that the United States is a republic, not in the sense of representative democracy, but as government by law instead of by majority opinion. The Constitution is seen as a kind of barrier between majority will and what the majority can impose. It protects the rights of minorities and places limits on change; but most important, it provides the society with the stability of law. For the NRPR, law is ultimately God's law, not a human creation. Since the Constitution is interpreted as the embodiment of biblical law, order, and morality in the American enterprise, the Constitution and the republic which it empowers are deposits of divinely granted authority. The NRPR, in effect, assumes that if it wins agreement on the point that the United States is a republic, and hence government by law, the only conceivable law upon which the entire operation could be based is the Word of God, which the NRPR, in turn, claims to read correctly. In language used earlier, this is *prescriptive* morality, calling for the imposition of what is *right* upon the nation, rather than for a common quest for what is *good*.

It is curious that despite the NRPR's ideological rejection, it gives much energy to the cultivation of participatory democracy. Voter registration, publication of voting records at both national and local levels, and the general effort to raise the level of political awareness on the part of the NRPR constituency mark an opening up of the democratic processes to those who previously had been on the fringes. Additionally, the attempt to elect certain candidates (or representatives of certain positions) to lawmaking offices indicates a practical affirmation of "majority rule." Once there are enough pro-family, pro-God, pro-moral, pro-American (etc.) people in public office, or in other words, once the majority has coalesced and won positions of power, the rule of biblically based law (what is *right*) can be achieved.

Since the NRPR view of the state differs so radically from that currently prevailing in the society, the crusade to instill it will certainly not go unchallenged. Perhaps what should be most hoped for here is that the debate be reasonable and civil. One of the more reasoned critiques of the NRPR's concept of the state has been leveled by David Little of the University of Virginia. Speaking to a Washington conference sponsored by the (conservative) Ethics and Public Policy Center, Little argued that the NRPR position on government and the public order is characterized by three basic propositions: (a) that public morality can and will be legislated; (b) that public morality can be imposed by majority vote; and (c) that public morality must be biblically based.[9]

On the first point, Little agreed with the NRPR, and properly so in our view, that morality indeed is continually legislated. We would add to the argument that legislation is but one dimension of the public order in which whatever morality there is resides. For organisms as complex and physiologically devoid of instinct as human beings, morality is either taught or its emergence is accidental. The faith that morality can be legislated may well be a harbinger of a wider faith that we can cooperatively mold ourselves and our children to be more responsible citizens.

Little, however, took issue with the second and third points of the NRPR's political stance. We have noted already that the NRPR's position on majority rule (the second point) is more complex than most critics (including Little) have realized. Still, as far as NRPR action is concerned, Little's argument seems accurate. (Interestingly, his argument against majority rule is much the same as that of the NRPR.) Little claimed that it is necessary to "test the credentials of consensus"—in short, that the opinions of that majority need to be judged by a higher criterion than mere numbers. Majority opinion may well be irrational or even perverse. Consequently, Little argued, there must be some minimum standards of rationality, coherence, consistency, and respect for the rules of relevance when one speaks in the political realm.

On the third point—biblical morality—the issue is clear-cut and does not require much attention. Here the NRPR promotes a highly sectarian reading of the Bible as normative civil law. However, a wide diversity of opinion exists within American Christianity on how the Bible is to be read, and also on its proper relationship to the public order. For the most part, the dominant religious groups in America have been in basic agreement with Thomas Jefferson on the proper relationship between faith and reason in the American political system: "Truth is great and will prevail if left to herself [and unless] disarmed of her natural weapons, free argument and debate."[10]

This Jeffersonian faith in reason represents a dimension of the founding fathers which the NRPR would rather ignore. Given the

NRPR's radical distrust of reason, its dismay at human autonomy, and its damning of humanism, one should not be surprised that America's Enlightenment heritage is slighted. In some ways this represents one of the most fundamental conflicts between the NRPR and the rest of society, for it encompasses the basic rules of the game—rules that determine what counts, what is relevant, what can be assumed, how we act in our shared reality. The NRPR has made skillful use of the Left's concept of cultural relativity in this argument, claiming, for example, that since science is a belief-system and hence a faith, it can have no more weight in the public realm than any other faith, particularly the Christian revelation. For the theological leaders of the NRPR, the Christian revelation, which exists in written form, is prior to and has inherent authority over the scientific endeavor. The turning of science upon the Scriptures, therefore, constitutes a blatant example of the arrogance of sin. The Bible is a given, an entity "above the fray," not a subject for form criticism or other device of secular humanism.

We have seen that the NRPR is recognizably quite convention-ally Christian in many of its teachings. It does embark on its own separate course, however, at some critical points. To us, the most critical point is that the NRPR would like to require that all participants in the public life of the society acknowledge the Truth—the particular understanding of religion and politics taught by American Fundamentalism.

CHAPTER 4

Organization, Structure, and Impact

Organizationally, the NRPR is a virtual labyrinth of political action committees, lobbies, educational and research foundations, publications, television programs, and churches. *Family and Freedom Digest,* published by Fletcher Brothers' Grace Community Chapel, is perhaps the single best directory of the NRPR. The *Digest* lists some ninety organizations, from Moral Majority, to The National Pro-Life Political Action Committee, to the Interfaith Committee Against Blasphemy. The widespread and sophisticated use of computerized mailing systems has allowed these groups to keep track of a vast number of members and potential donors. Membership in most involves a donation, usually in the $10 to $25 range, part of which buys one a subscription to the group's newsletter, newspaper, or similar publication.

Part of the membership of the NRPR thus "exists" in the memory banks of direct-mail computers. Lists of donors are commonly shared, or bought and sold, so that placement on one organization's mailing list often brings mailings from other NRPR organizations. This system has several advantages. It allows particular groups to contact likely supporters while reducing the risk of waste, since a supporter of one NRPR cause is likely to support others as well. Computerization of the process also allows a group to identify particular constituencies within its lists of members and likely supporters. It should be possible to identify and mail information to supporters in Putnam County, New York, or to locate people in southern Louisiana who have contributed to an antipornography appeal. The only limit may be the extent of ingenuity exercised in organizing and cross-referencing the information obtained.

But drawbacks do exist. Many groups are attracting support from the same constituency. Generous donors are likely to be deluged by appeals from new causes, as well as ones already supported, far beyond their ability to respond with financial contributions. The people involved in these operations realize that such duplication and overkill are wasteful, but there seems to be little chance of avoiding it, given the number of groups seeking support and the wide circulation of duplicated mailing lists. Direct-mail fund raising has been the object of attention, much of it focusing on the high cost, since the appearance of the New Right. A large mailing might cost several hundred thousand dollars, just to cover expenses. It will, however, generate a list of donors who can be solicited a second time at a much lower cost and with a much higher return. Additionally, even the break-even mailing gets the group's message out, usually in an emotionally charged fashion. While the mailing might not always find donors, it might yield some sympathizers. But there is always the risk that constant appeals for financial support will ultimately alienate a constituency. One of the more common complaints against organized religion that we hear voiced by college students is still its pitch for money. Our explanations that the churches are in the world, and that unless one likes worshiping in the rain, finances always will be important to church life, meet with only grudging acknowledgment.

Religious Right fund raising is only occasionally low-key. More often it is rather high pressure, equating success for a particular dollar amount with a victory for God. Usually the whole enterprise of a television ministry will be portrayed as standing on the brink of disaster without significant *immediate* support. For example, here are portions of an April 1981 mailing by the "Old-Time Gospel Hour" (OTGH):

It now appears that, after 25 years of broadcasting and televising the gospel, the Old-Time Gospel Hour may go off the air.

We can no longer survive the pressures caused by increased costs. . . . Every television station and radio station which carries the Old-Time Gospel Hour is in immediate jeopardy of being cut off the air.

Is there any hope for continuing the Old-Time Gospel Hour? The only hope we have is to raise $3 million in the next few days. . . .

I am asking you . . . for a sacrificial gift of $25. This is a last ditch effort. We are asking God for a miracle. We cannot go into the month of June without a supernatural intervention.

The fund-raising letter just cited followed, by two weeks, an appeal for a $15 donation for World Hunger Day, billed as "the Christian answer to the communists' May Day." That venture asked for only a total of $100,000 for Food for the Hungry International. It was noted that contributions would also support other work of the OTGH. These two pleas went out about the same time as a mailing seeking new "faith-partners" for the OTGH. A promise to donate $10 a month obtained for one the Faith-Partners Bible; "a monthly letter sharing my [Jerry Falwell's] feeling on issues too hot for me to talk about on television"; and two bronze Jesus First pins, among other things. A later May Rally Day mailing repeated the danger that the OTGH might vanish from the airwaves. This letter was more personalized than the earlier version, threatening that the program would be lost in the letter recipient's particular area. A gift of $25 was again the suggested amount. Early June 1981 saw a mailing soliciting $10 to support a campaign against the teaching of evolution. This in turn was followed by a mid-June letter seeking $150,000 for a Food for the Hungry relief mission to Southeast Asian boat people. Donations again were to be shared with OTGH. A week later, Moral Majority members received a request for a special donation to further the work already accomplished.

As success breeds imitation, those contributing to NRPR causes will find themselves increasingly hard-pressed to support over-lapping and frequently competitive organizations. The mass ministries which supply some of the basic cohesiveness of the

NRPR may need to worry about being captured by the logic of economic expansion. It is ironic to note that despite Falwell's condemnation of deficit spending by the federal government, the OTGH is depicted in its mailings as $5 million in debt and several months behind in meeting its bills. In fact, a 1980 audit found the Falwell empire some $19 million in debt. Falwell's financial difficulties have received extensive attention in the press. At one point, the "Old-Time Gospel Hour" was placed in receivership and forced to rescind a $6 million bond issue. Invariably on the brink of financial disaster, owing to a "God will provide" attitude, Falwell has thus far avoided collapse through his mastery of fund raising. By no means is Falwell's OTGH the only media ministry seeking emergency support. This is a widespread fact of life in an era of expensive technology and expanding markets.

The OTGH fund-raising appeal to counter the teaching of evolution is significant in that it demonstrates the variety of active organizations in the NRPR and their interconnections. Most Americans probably date their knowledge of the term political action committee (PAC) from the 1980 elections. The PACs are only a few of a number of suborganizations within the NRPR. The existence of PACs was encouraged by changes in the election laws which limited the amount of money any individual or organization (including PACs) could contribute to a candidate, but left unlimited the amount of money a PAC could spend in an "independent campaign"—a campaign either for or against a candidate, but one which has no official ties to any campaign organization.

Political action committees therefore have been useful in circumventing the limitations placed on campaign contributions by the election laws. However, they can be expensive. They are not tax-exempt, and the contributions they receive are not tax-deductible. An individual can receive a tax credit for up to $50 for contributions to a PAC, but for contributions above that amount, any such advantage ceases. (A tax-credit reduces one's taxes directly; a tax-deduction reduces one's taxable income.) Lobbies, by contrast, are tax-exempt, although contributions to a lobby are not tax-deductible. While lobbies cannot involve themselves in campaigns, their areas of operation often overlap those of the PAC. Still more economical is the "educational foundation," essentially a research and publication organization, which is both tax-exempt and tax-deductible. The least expensive way to finance political efforts is with money which receives the greatest tax "break." Consequently, it makes little sense for a PAC to lobby (seek to influence legislation), or for either a PAC or a lobbying organization to engage in research-educational ventures, since the activities in question can be more economically performed by less-taxed entities. This has led to the proliferation of different branches of what is ultimately the same organization. Christian Voice (CV), most widely known for its Congressional "report cards" and its independent Christians for Reagan campaign, is legally three different organizations. Christian Voice, the lobby, is tax-exempt and can legally attempt to influence legislation, but it cannot participate directly in electoral politics without losing its tax-exempt status. The Christian Voice PAC, the Christian Voice Moral Government Fund, is not tax-exempt and can participate in electoral politics. Some of the research necessary for Christian Voice and CV-PAC to operate effectively, however, can be supported by The Christian Voice Fund, CV's educational foundation.

During the early part of the campaign, Moral Majority operated a PAC which made direct contributions to campaigns. A Baptist minister known to us received $1,000 from the Moral Majority PAC in his unsuccessful bid for state legislator in his party's primary. Moral Majority later backed away from such direct involvement in campaigns; the PAC was dissolved and a policy of nonendorsement of political candidates was announced. This shift in policy, however, did not appreciably diminish Moral Majority's ability to make an impact on elections—it just made the impact less expensive. In actual fact, Moral Majority's nonendorsement policy seems to apply to explicit endorsement and direct support only. Moral Majority appears to have learned that it could be just as effective through its lobby (Moral Majority), its educational foundation (The Moral Majority Fund), and the "Old-Time Gospel Hour," as it could through a PAC.

To illustrate: The issue of *Moral Majority Report* which carried the article "Why Moral Majority Does Not Endorse Candidates," also contained two articles critical of Jimmy Carter (one associated Carter with the gay-rights movement; the other claimed the White House was attempting to manipulate the Evangelical vote). The same issue carried articles critical of Senators Edward Kennedy and Alan Cranston, and three articles favorable to Moral Majority-approved candidates (without explicit endorsement of those candidates).[1] This pattern held constant throughout the course of the election. Articles favorable to Jeremiah Denton, now a United States Senator from Alabama, Representative Henry Hyde (R–Ill.), and most prominently, Ronald Reagan, appeared in the pages of *Moral Majority Report*. The only articles we have seen on the then incumbent President associated Carter with the White House Conference on the Family, opposition to organized prayer in public schools, and a liberal position on gay rights, all unlikely to gain Carter much favor with the Moral Majority's constituency.

Similarly, during the numerous "I Love America" rallies which Falwell held across the country, he was able to make nonendorsements (that is, nonexplicit endorsements) of favored candidates simply by sharing the podium or introducing them as persons committed to pro-moral stances, while mentioning that their opponents had unfortunately, or misguidedly, voted for disapproved legislation such as the ERA. When the July 30, 1980, edition of *Moral Majority Report* carried a picture of Ronald Reagan and Jerry Falwell on its cover and, inside, pictures of Reagan with Falwell, with Phyllis Schlafly, with Jerry Prevo (Moral Majority director in Alaska), and with Howard Phillips (national director of the Conservative Caucus), an endorsement would have been superfluous.

Ultimately, the distinction among NRPR lobbies, PACs, and educational foundations may amount to little more than separate bank accounts. They employ the same people (or often hire them as consultants, paying them with the appropriate funds), share mailing lists and office space, and divide up the process of supporting a candidate or an issue so that they can get the most for their money. The fund-raising letter mailed by the "Old-Time Gospel Hour" to combat the teaching of evolution allows much of the expense of what already is, at some points, a lobbying and campaign effort to be borne by a tax-exempt organization, donations to which are tax-deductible.

While NRPR organizations are similar at the level of national fund raising, marked differences prevail at other levels. Shared political goals and moral positions have expressed themselves in various kinds of structures. One useful way to distinguish between NRPR organizations is by noting the degree to which the central structure dominates in each. Let us suggest two heuristic extremes: (a) the professional-lobby type organization, controlled by a small number of key figures who set the agenda for the organization as a whole and who determine what will take place in local areas; (b) the grass-roots type organization, with agenda set locally and not under the control of the central figures. It is important to be aware that any real organization will display a bit of each of these styles. The distinction is ultimately one of emphasis. A second way to differentiate NRPR organizations is by the extent to which they have become directly involved in mobilizing masses of conservative Christian voters. Some groups have thrown themselves zealously into this effort while others have served primarily as vehicles for motivating and training community leaders. We might apply a traditional mass/elite distinction here, remembering again that it will not be unusual for groups to do a bit of each. Two organizations highly active in the 1980 elections serve to illustrate our first distinction, centraliza-tion—Christian Voice and Moral Majority. Both would fall also under the "mass contact" side of the second distinction. The Religious Roundtable provides a clear example of an organization primarily for elites.

Christian Voice

Although it includes a lobby, a PAC, and an educational foundation, Christian Voice is one of the smaller NRPR organizations. It has claimed some forty thousand clerical members, and perhaps three times as many lay members, but these represent primarily contributors and recipients of material rather than ongoing local organizations. At its center, CV employed about seven people, most as consultants. The organization began in California in 1978 at the time of the battle over Proposition 6, which would have limited homosexual rights (the proposition failed). The CV's national headquarters are still located in Pacific Grove, California, and its mailing operation is carried on from Pasadena. In 1979, CV opened up a legislative office in Washington, D.C., met with conservative Christian and political figures, and extended invitations to join its advisory board. A 1980 CV publication lists fifteen congressional advisors, including some well-known names: Senators Orrin G. Hatch, Gordon Humphrey, and Roger Jepson; Representatives Daniel Crane, Robert Dorman, and George Hansen. Christian Voice participated in several lobbying campaigns: It helped maintain the tax-exempt status of Christian schools, joined in defeating legislation which would have prohibited discrimination on the basis of sexual preference, and made an (unsuccessful) effort to get a bill allowing school prayer out of committee and onto the floor of the House.

Perhaps the most notable CV project during the 1980 campaign was its direct partisan political activity carried out through its PAC, the Christian Voice Moral Government Fund (CVMGF). Unlike Moral Majority, CVMGF explicitly endorsed candidates and offered its assistance to candidates' campaign committees. It targeted some thirty-six incumbents for defeat (all but one of them Democrats) and in each race, sent a letter to the challenger's campaign committee outlining its strategy. The CVMGF informed the challengers that it would be preparing voting-record flyers "documenting how the targeted incumbent has consistently voted against our interests on important moral/family issues," and distributing them "to Christians as they leave Sunday church services." Candidates were informed that their workers could distribute CVMGF material; that where it was able, CVMGF would donate the material as an "in kind" contribution to the campaign; and that candidates could purchase CVMGF material, or they could duplicate it from CVMGF-supplied "photo-ready boards" at their own expense. The CVMGF also requested names of likely workers from the candidate's own campaign or from conservative churches, and lists of local conservative publications.[2]

Prior to launching its campaign efforts, CV had worked hard at identifying and recruiting conservative Christian ministers. This effort continued for the duration of the campaign. Christian Voice sent out a fifteen-page recruiting packet, containing an account of the nation's moral failings; biblical passages enjoining political action; quotations from leading political figures, past and present, pointing to the centrality of religion in America; and descriptions of its objectives. The material was written for conservative Christians who are in agreement on a central body of moral issues, but who also are reticent about political involvement. Christian Voice thus worked at mobilizing a hitherto unorganized and nonparticipating segment of the population. The material consequently argued that both America and Christianity were in grave danger from common enemies and that political action was a religious obligation.

> What a powerful witness to our work on behalf of the Kingdom of God in this nation founded "under God" and populated by a Christian majority. We have stood aside and allowed the forces of Satan to govern our people and to take control of the shape of our destiny.
> These are not political issues—liberal vs. conservative or Democrat vs. Republican. We are not concerned with energy policies, farm subsidies, economic or political theory, etc.
> *These are moral issues*—good vs. evil, Christ vs. anti-Christ.[3]

At the national level, Christian Voice ran a Christians for Reagan campaign, involving several kinds of advertising. Some two million *Make Your Christian Vote Count* pamphlets were distributed, claiming: "Ronald Reagan is the only candidate that has firmly stood behind his Christian principles at the risk of political loss. The American Christian Community must support Ronald Reagan for President in 1980." The bulk of the pamphlet reproduced portions of George Otis' 1976 interview with Reagan on a syndicated TV program, "High Adventure." Otis is a conservative Christian businessman, once president of Lear Jet Corporation and the honorary chairman of Christians for Reagan. Calling it The Faith of Ronald Reagan, the pamphlet presented Reagan's bicentennial call for Americans "to reclaim those great principles embodied in [the] Judeo-Christian tradition and in ancient Scripture." Also presented was Reagan's claim to be born again ("In my own experience there came a time when there developed a new relationship with God") and his promise to "call upon God for help" if elected to "the job in Washington." The full interview with Otis was aired on some two hundred Christian television and radio stations across the country.

On the side of negative campaigning, the CV strategy was to attempt to erode Carter's support among southern Evangelicals whom CV feared would vote for Carter "from regional pride or Christian brotherhood."[4] To this end, the CVMGF prepared two television ads associating Carter with advocacy of gay rights and several other emotionally charged issues. Carter was indeed vulnerable here, since his position paper submitted to the Democratic platform committee read:

> We must affirm the dignity of all people and the right of each individual to have equal access to and participation in the institutions and services of our society, including actions to protect all groups from discrimination based on race, color, religion, national origin, sex or sexual orientation.

The transcript of one CVMGF television ad ran as follows:

> Militant homosexuals parade in San Francisco, flaunting their lifestyle. Flexing their political muscle, they elect a mayor.
>
> Homosexuals in New York City. They, too, elect a mayor.
>
> Now the march has reached Washington.
>
> And President Carter's platform carries his pledge to cater to homosexual demands.
>
> The choice November fourth involves moral issues.
>
> Carter advocates acceptance of homosexuality.
>
> Ronald Reagan stands for the traditional American Family.

And the second ad was in the same vein:

> As a Christian mother, I want my children to be able to pray in school. I don't want them being taught that abortion and homosexuality are perfectly alright.

I was very sorry to learn that President Carter disagrees with me on all of these issues. Because of this, I'm duty bound as a Christian and a mother to vote for Ronald Reagan, a man that will protect my family's values.[5]

Both ads ended with: "This message has been brought to you by Christians for Reagan, a project of the Christian Voice Moral Government Fund." Originally scheduled to run on at least five stations, the ads apparently were presented only in Memphis, Tennessee, and in Greenville, South Carolina. However, that was sufficient for them to be picked up by the national news media, where they gained extensive free coverage.

At more local levels—that is, Senate and House races—CV distributed Congressional report cards, often assisting in building the organizations to make that possible. Virtually all the campaign organizations contacted by CV welcomed its support and, in many cases, distributed CV literature; occasionally they reprinted it themselves and used CV volunteers for phone banks and other duties. The basic work for the report cards was done by the lobby and involved going through the votes of the Ninety-sixth Congress (1978-80) to select issues likely to appeal to the CV constituency. Christian Voice printed the *Congressional Report Card* which presented the votes of every member of the House and Senate on such selected issues as Taiwan security, sex and racial quotas, aid for Marxist Nicaragua, Salt II, and forced school busing. These more specialized topics supplemented the usual issues of sex education, school prayer, abortion, and private schools. Since the *Report Card* covered a relatively wide range of votes and included all Senators and Representatives, it could legally be printed and distributed by CV, the lobbying organization. For particular Congressional races, the CVMGF printed small report cards which compared incumbent and challenger on six or seven issues geared to particular local concerns.

A glimpse at one case should prove illuminating. The report card of John Culver of Iowa (defeated by CV-supported Charles Grassley) gave seven "failing grades" to the liberal Democrat. The Culver votes recorded were: (a) against prayer in schools; (b) against parental consent for sex education; (c) for busing to achieve racial integration; (d) for Medicaid abortion funds; (e) against freeing Christian schools from Internal Revenue scrutiny; (f) against requiring a balanced budget; and (g) against a motion to *limit* abortion funds. The first five votes recorded were on measures proposed by Senator Jesse Helms (R–N.C.), the leading political figure of the New Right. Of the remaining two, the budget measure was a Roth (of Kemp-Roth tax-cutting fame) proposal, and the second abortion vote was on a Richard Schweiker motion (Schweiker is now Reagan's Secretary of Health and Human Services). Report cards produced for House races were substantially the same, usually substituting a vote on "cutbacks on humanist research" for the Senate's vote on private schools.

The introductory copy on the report cards was the same for both Senate and House. A large NO in inch-high letters appeared next to a picture of the targeted incumbent, "Your man in Congress ————." Below, the message read:

> We do not believe that America's Christians will remain silent while the country continues its slide toward national suicide! . . . America was founded by men of faith on godly principles. . . . A return to moral accountability . . . is imperative if we, as a nation, are to survive. . . . We cannot . . . rely on ungodly men and women to preserve this nation. . . . (Incumbent's name) deserves your prayers—but not your votes.

In some instances the CVMGF printed tabloid-size vote comparisons pitting Reagan against Carter, and the favored congressional challenger against an incumbent. These report cards also contained a reprint of The Faith of Ronald Reagan.

In order to get its message out to potential voters, CV employed a number of tactics. Each campaign supported by CV received 1,000 CVMGF report cards, master forms for making duplicates, and lists of CV ministers in the district. The approximately 40,000 ministers belonging to CV also received report cards which they were asked to reproduce and distribute. In addition, these ministers were encouraged to preach (a) on the Christian responsibility to register and vote, and (b) on the moral issues used by CV in its report cards.

In some instances, particularly in those races where media

coverage created test cases, CV made some extensive organizational efforts. Rallies brought together a variety of conservative speakers and helped identify and inspire potential CV workers. Since the purpose of rallies can be substantially educational, CV often was able to pay for them out of its lobby funds rather than from its PAC money, which it would have had to report as an in-kind contribution to a campaign. In Iowa, where CV planned to spend more than the $5,000 limit on PAC contributions to a single candidate, it established Christians for Grassley to run its independent expenditure campaign. Various CV leaders traveled around the country, concentrating particularly on Iowa, Idaho, Indiana, and Colorado. Their major job was to create loosely structured organizations to distribute CV material at churches on the Sunday before election day. Christian Voice proved adept at cooperating with other NRPR groups and at facilitating cooperation among them. Pro-life groups, Moral Majority, Eagle Forum, conservative political organizations, Fundamentalists, charismatics, in one case the John Birch Society, and in some other cases local Republican party organizations—all were drawn into collaboration by the CV effort. This handful of CV leaders reminds us of the circuit riders of the heyday of frontier evangelization. They would arrive in a community, provide some inspiration and training, help create the rudiments of an organization, and then move on. In retrospect, CV claims an impact on twenty-two races in the 1980 election, including some fairly big names: John Culver, George McGovern, Frank Church, and Birch Bayh. During the brief hiatus before the next election, CV will continue its lobbying efforts, primarily in Washington, D.C.

Moral Majority

The most visible and best known of the NRPR groups, Moral Majority, Inc., has been equated in the mind of most Americans with the whole of this kind of religious/political activity. People who are somewhat unsure about what one might mean by "new religious/political Right," receive instant enlightenment as soon as one adds "like Moral Majority." Of all the organized groups comprising the NRPR, Moral Majority (MM) strikes us as the most interesting organizationally, and potentially the most enduring. At the national level, MM entails a number of distinct suborganizations. Moral Majority itself is a lobby, similar to Christian Voice. As such, it is tax-exempt, but donations to it are not tax-deductible (MM is one of the few organizations in the NRPR which clearly indicates on its literature that gifts are not tax-deductible). In addition, there are The Moral Majority Foundation, MM's "educational foundation"; and the Moral Majority Legal Defense Foundation, which provides legal services to those "pro-moral organizations who are attacked by the godless, amoral forces of humanism."[6] Both of these may receive tax-deductible contributions. For a short while, MM operated a PAC which became dormant early in the 1980 campaign, but not before making contributions totaling more than $20,000 to selected campaigns. Jerry Falwell, the president and founder, has come to embody MM, if not the entire NRPR, in his own person. One of MM's strengths is that it is headed by a man who must be acknowledged as the nation's most charismatic religious leader.

Like Christian Voice, MM also has attempted to build an ecumenical political organization. Ideally, it would like to be even more ecumenical than CV by avoiding an explicitly Christian self-presentation. The MM recruitment letter, except for identifying Jerry Falwell with the "Old-Time Gospel Hour," displays little explicit connection to Christianity. In the "civil religion" style (see chapter 6), it appeals merely to "God," without hinting at Trinitarianism. Its theme is that "the grand old flag is going down the drain," a phrase repeated seven times. Like its CV counterpart, it enumerates signs of decay, but MM focuses more on sins of the flesh—homosexuality and pornography accounting for four of the first five listed. The letter charges "amoral liberals" with "trying to corrupt our nation" and "giving in to the Communists," but offers the hope that God is not "finished with America" and that MM can "turn this nation around" before God abandons us. The letter is written in the first person, reflecting MM's close identification with Jerry Falwell, in contrast to the third-person style used in Christian Voice literature.[7]

Moral Majority certainly contains some non-Christian members, although how many, we cannot ascertain. We suspect the number is fairly small, and we base that guess upon two factors. First, the MM directory of state leaders (published in *Moral Majority Report* (2/1 [January 19, 1981], and already somewhat out of date in June 1981) is filled with church names such as Quint City Baptist Temple, Heritage Baptist Church, and Open Door Baptist Church. Many leaders not identified in the listing with specific congregations are nevertheless identifiable as pastors of independent Fundamentalist churches, often Baptist. Accounts of the growth of MM chapters throughout the country—regularly printed in earlier *Reports*—follow the same pattern.

Second, *Moral Majority Report,* in its religiously oriented articles, has published only material evidencing a clearly conservative Christian position. It consistently has argued that *Christians* have a right to participate in the political realm, that *Christians* are "coming out of their closets" to become a potent political force, that *Christians* are threatened by the growing secularity of American society. Although MM welcomes Jewish members, and indeed is particularly happy to gain Jewish participation, when the *Report* has considered American Jews, it has done so only when calling for support of Israel. The fact that mainline and liberal Protestants are seldom mentioned in the *Report,* except negatively in stories critical of the National Council of Churches, leads one to interpret *Christian,* when used positively, to mean generally *Evangelical Protestant,* and more specifically, *Fundamentalist.*

Thus although MM can claim a fairly broad membership, appealing to Americans of various faiths who share its political and moral concerns, it is also clear that its basic ongoing organizational strength comes from a particular segment of American churches. Given this dimension, we are inclined to suggest that MM may well be functioning as the denominational body of independent Fundamentalist congregations, or perhaps as their "national council of churches." Certainly it has helped break down the isolation in which those churches have traditionally served the Lord, granted them access to the public world, and given them a sense of organized collaboration with like-minded Christians.

Although Jerry Falwell has been by far the leading religious figure of the NRPR, virtually eclipsing all other luminaries, MM's operation has been rather astonishingly independent of his leadership. Falwell's assistance probably was vital in the establishment of local MM organizations throughout the country. His I Love America and America You're Too Young to Die rallies (many of the latter were carried on independently of Falwell) gave significant impetus to the development of state organizations. Yet our conversations with MM leaders around the country have indicated that, in a sense, MM existed before Falwell, after being approached by New Right leaders, began his organizational efforts. In many cases conservative pastors had been meeting together for some time, sharing their concerns about societal decay and looking for ways to counter it. What MM did, then, was to galvanize incipient organizations and provide them with a way to achieve some self-identity and cohesiveness, as well as enable them to move from a position of alienation to center stage in the national political drama.

Like Christian Voice, MM put a good deal of effort into organizing during the 1980 elections—setting up state branches and something like county coordinators within each state. The precise form of organization was, and still is, quite flexible. In some states MM is structured on a county basis, with a key figure in each county being in close touch with the state organization. In other states MM is structured by election districts, and in still others, by population centers; some even mix these styles. These patterns indicate a pragmatic attitude—they use the style that works best in each case. Parallels to this organizational freedom are evident in other dimensions of MM. State organizations generally have been quite independent of the national MM. During the 1980 elections, voting records were printed and distributed by a large number of state MM offices. They dealt with contests for the state legislature and the county, township, and city offices, as well as the Presidential and Congressional races.

Some of the organizations listed in the *Report* as members of the national MM actually deny any official connection with the national organization. One has the feeling that many of these people are fiercely independent and that while they agree with

Jerry Falwell on most matters and are willing to cooperate extensively with him and support him, they should not be dismissed as mere extensions of his will. They have their own concerns and issues, although these tend to be compatible with those of the national organization. We were taken aback when one of the MM leaders in Kansas told us that his organization was doing nothing, but we recovered from shock when he provided the explanation, "Kansas is so conservative there's nothing for us to do." Even some of the embarrassments suffered by MM—and rather gleefully reported by the news media—can be read as indications of local autonomy. The MM leader arrested for soliciting homosexual sex with minors, and the action taken by another against genitally complete gingerbread people—using undercover children, according to some accounts—may be instances of bad eggs or of trifling extremism, but they also illustrate the fact that the local MM was not on a leash. (The people involved in these instances were later dismissed from MM.)

It is the existence of ongoing state and local organizations that distinguishes MM from other NRPR organizations. Although CV also worked at the grass-roots level, the cooperative endeavors it created do not appear to have the staying power of those of MM. Moral Majority is capable of offering its members at local levels not a counterculture, but an alternative society: networks which connect churches to each other; public forums for the discussion of issues; the possibility that people hitherto either excluded from or without access to the public world can now begin to shape it and can bear the responsibility for those actions. The autonomy of MM subgroups may also increase the chances for discussions and negotiation with those in the center or on the Left. Nationally, the battle lines tend to be drawn as if between the light and the darkness. National enemies often are vague as well as menacing— secular humanism, international communism, liberalism. Locally, however, one is more likely to be drawn into conflict with people who are one's neighbors, even friends.

For the national causes and concerns, MM provided its members with extensive resources. Falwell's rallies drew a great deal of media attention and certainly spurred interest. Again like CV, MM found it necessary to encourage political involvement on the part of conservative Christians. Leadership training sessions, primarily for interested ministers, and run in conjunction with the Committee for the Survival of a Free Congress, provided the basis of political action. In this same vein, *MM Report* printed information on actions churches could legally take in the way of political activity.[8] For example, it is perfectly legal for a minister to endorse a political candidate from the pulpit on Sunday morning, as long as he does so as an individual and not as an official spokesman for the church. Candidates for public office may legally appear and speak at services, or at other times, as long as the same privilege is open to all candidates. As corporate groups, churches may engage in lobbying efforts, as long as they do not spend more than about 5 percent of their income on such activities. (For some of the larger churches around the nation, 5 percent can amount to a considerable sum.) Churches may register voters, sometimes right in the church, depending upon local registration procedures. Indeed, voter registration was one of the major activities of churches associated with MM during the 1980 campaign.

In addition to such practical assistance, the *Moral Majority Report* provided its subscribers with continuing coverage of various issues and activities involving MM. During the period between January and November 1980, the topics that appeared most frequently in the *Report* included pornography, school prayer and curriculum, abortion, Christian political activity, and MM's self-explanations. Readers were also kept abreast of Falwell's various activities, as well as some of the activities of other NRPR groups. Extensive coverage was given to Menachem Begin's meeting with eight conservative pastors (including Falwell, Adrian Rogers, Charles Stanley, James Kennedy, and Greg Dixon); to MM participation in the Virginia Republican Convention; to several MM conventions; to a New Jersey housewife's battle against a public school sex-education program; and to various pieces of legislation either supported or opposed by MM. The general tone of *MM Report* is a kind of defensive triumphalism. While there are grave dangers in the world in the form of genetic research, sexual freedom, liberal legislation, and the like, the *Report* announces that the people of God (or those of godly morals) have arrived in the public arena *with power*. We are a force to be reckoned with; we have already accomplished great things and we will continue to do so, is their message.

The Roundtable

Founded by conservative Christian businessman Edward McAteer, the Roundtable (sometimes known as the Religious Roundtable, or the Christian Roundtable) has served primarily as an agency to coordinate and provide resources for conservative religious leaders. The Roundtable had its day in the sun at the National Affairs Briefing in Dallas in August 1980. There is little doubt that this was one of the central events in catapulting the NRPR into the national consciousness. The appearance of their presidential aspirant, Reagan, who endorsed "the old-time gospel" and "the old-time Constitution," and the comments of Bailey Smith that God does not hear the prayers of Jews, won the briefing extensive, albeit controversial coverage. The Dallas meeting attracted a crowd of some 18,000 people. This was by far the best-attended Roundtable event.

In a *Conservative Digest* interview, McAteer claimed that the Roundtable provided "educational material to over 40,000 people" between August and November of 1980, a rather small number when compared to the efforts of Moral Majority.[9] This comment should not be taken as depreciation of Roundtable activities, since, unlike Christian Voice and Moral Majority, the Roundtable is not a mass-mobilization organization. Its work is primarily with and for leaders—the elite of the NRPR. In the same *Conservative Digest* interview, McAteer made two points clear:

> When you get one pastor who is oriented along the lines we're talking about, who is prepared to articulate the positions properly, who knows what the issues are and what they mean, when you get one person like that then of course you multiply your effectiveness. We stress leadership, getting these leaders together.[10]

Perhaps the best illustration of this method was the Roundtable's National Leadership Seminar held in Washington, D.C., in January 1980, in conjunction with the National Religious Broadcasters and National Association of Evangelicals convention. The meeting featured brief presentations by a host of leading figures from the NRPR, as well as from the secular New Right. Richard Viguerie, Paul Weyrich (Committee for the Survival of a Free Congress [CSFC]), Terry Dolan (National Conservative Political Action Committee [NCPAC]), Howard Phillips (The Conservative Caucus), and Senators Jesse Helms, Gordon Humphrey, and Roger Jepson shared the spotlight with such "civilians" as Jerry Falwell and Tim LaHaye of Moral Majority. The board of directors of the Roundtable overlaps the executive board of Moral Majority, and its Council of 56 includes some well-known New Right politicians and NRPR leaders, as well as such lesser-known figures as E. V. Hill, pastor of Mt. Zion Missionary Baptist Church, Los Angeles; Clay Claiborne of Black Silent Majority; and Douglas Peterson of the Christian Studies Center. The Roundtable, then, serves as a contact point for a variety of NRPR leaders and, additionally, appears to be one of the key instruments for keeping the NRPR and the nonreligious New Right in touch with each other.

Like other NRPR organizations, the Roundtable publishes a newsletter. The *Roundtable Report* is aimed principally at pastors and provides information on how to procure copies of House or Senate bills, how to check on the status of legislation, and how to have oneself invited to testify before a Congressional committee, as well as information on significant pending legislation and where to write in order to influence it. During the 1980 campaign the Roundtable distributed a manual on organizing a church for political activity. The manual includes information on different voter registration procedures around the country and suggests a way churches can identify unregistered members. (The minister should have the entire congregation stand and then ask all those registered to sit down; those remaining on their feet then receive voter registration information from the church's "moral action chairman.") Also provided are the addresses of Christian Voice and the National Christian Action Coalition, from whom the church can obtain information on the way their representatives voted on various issues. The manual concludes with instructions on how to get out the vote on election day, a synopsis of Moral Majority's information on the sort of political activity that legally can be engaged in by a church, and a sample questionnaire for churches to send to candidates. Unlike all other NRPR material, this undated manual, titled *A Program for Political Participation of Church-Going Christians,* carries no identification as to who produced it. The reason, according to a CV lobbyist, is that the manual was prepared by the Republican National Committee, a fact which would account for the anonymity and the sophistication of the instructions and further illustrate the Roundtable's function as an elite organization—"getting the leaders together."

A second valuable publication produced by the Roundtable was a guide to the American political system written by William Chasey, executive vice-president of the Roundtable's Governmental and Political Affairs division. In *The Legislative Scenario,* Chasey equipped readers with rudimentary information on the structure and operation of Congress—what the Senate and House are, how representatives are elected, how committees function, how a bill becomes a law, how to monitor the status of proposed legislation.[11] The fact that the Roundtable found it necessary to make such basic information available reflects the appalling ignorance of most Americans regarding our political system and stands as an indictment of the educational system, which has failed to provide citizens with even the minimum prerequisites for responsible political participation. All organizations of whatever ideological stripe would do well to avail themselves of material like this in a common effort to eliminate ignorance.

Some of the Roundtable's educational information came from The Plymouth Rock Foundation, a very conservative educational foundation which might fairly be described as right wing, even by NRPR standards. The distinguishing mark of the Plymouth Rock/Roundtable materials is the claim that positions on highly specific social, political, and economic issues are biblically based:

Inflation is anti-biblical—"Amos took the higher power to task for 'making the ephah small and the shekel great.'"

Progressive tax-rates are anti-biblical—"Each . . . head of household is to pay the same portion of income to support the government." (10-15%)

The presence of women in the armed forces is anti-biblical— "According to God's word, armies are to be composed of men only."[12]

Certainly materials of this sort are not unique to Plymouth Rock or to the Roundtable. However, the Plymouth Rock-produced material does illustrate in a particularly lucid way certain tendencies of NRPR literature—namely, its claim to rather global competence in dealing with issues and its confidence that clear biblical answers can be found for even the most difficult and complex social questions.

The Impact of the NRPR

A vast number of people would like to be able to assess the impact of the NRPR upon the 1980 elections. Unfortunately, no one can, at least not with a satisfying degree of accuracy. There has been considerable disagreement as to the NRPR's effect, a fact significant in itself, if one pays attention to who is saying what. Even such basic information as the number of voters registered by the NRPR is not likely ever to become available. Most of the state Moral Majority representatives with whom we talked said they simply did not know how many new voter registrations were produced by MM efforts. That many people were registered is beyond doubt. Nationally, the figure of NRPR registrations has been put at three to four million—but this is at best an educated guess. The unfortunate fact of the matter is that nobody counted. Just as frustrating is the unavailability of hard data for state and local elections. Countless state legislature, county commission, and school board contests probably were affected by the NRPR, but we cannot know how many, or how much.

Conversations with NRPR activists have revealed a tendency to assess their impact in rather modest terms. While the NRPR does believe it had an effect, this is usually expressed as influencing the size of a victory rather than as being the decisive factor. In only a few contests does the NRPR entertain the possibility that it may have made the difference between victory and defeat. In its evaluation of the fall 1980 elections, Christian Voice notes that of the thirty-six candidates it supported, twenty-two won, but it does not claim to have been decisive in that many contests. In numerous races where the NRPR was active, the New Right PACs (NCPAC, CSFC) also made substantial efforts, thus clouding the results even more.

Christian Voice does evaluate its effect as significant in the defeat of a number of liberals: in the Senate—Culver (D–Iowa) Church (D–Idaho), McGovern (D–S. Dak.), Bayh (D–Ind.), and Stewart (D–Ala.); in House races—Brademas (D–Ind.), Buchanan (Ala. Republican primary), Fisher and Harris (D–Va.), Eckhardt (D–Tex.), and Corman (D–Calif.). Winning Senate candidates supported by Moral Majority included John East (R–N.C.), Frank Murkowski (R–Alas.), Jeremiah Denton (R–Ala.), Paula Hawkins, (R–Fla.), Charles Grassley, (R–Iowa), Don Nichols (R–Okla.), Daniel Quayle, (R–Ind.), James Abdnor, (R–S. Dak.), Steven Symms (R–Idaho), Robert Dole (R–Kans.), and Paul Laxalt (R–Nev.). In the House, MM supported Albert Lee Smith (R–Ala.), Jack Fields (R–Tex.), and Frank Wolf (R–Va.), all winners. The NRPR suffered losses in races it considered significant in California, Colorado, Georgia, Arizona, Texas, and Maryland. This is hardly a complete list, but it does give some idea of the extent of NRPR activity. Simply the size of the voter turnout in the Alabama Republican primary in which Albert Lee Smith defeated John Buchanan is an indication of the NRPR's potential impact. In 1978, Buchanan won by approximately 9,000 votes to 7,000. In 1980, when he met defeat, the vote was 25,000 to 20,000.

Defeated candidates with whom we spoke have attributed a larger role to the NRPR than have the victors. Those who won tended to look on their opponents' assessment of NRPR effect as cases of scapegoating—"they had to blame it on someone"—but we think that interpretation is inaccurate. The people who seem most interested in attributing a powerful impact to the NRPR are those from the nonreligious Right (dare we say the New Non-RPR?). Perhaps these are cases of courting what is perceived as a valuable constituency. Whatever the motivation, *Conservative Digest* printed articles contending that the NRPR was *the* deciding factor in a large number of races; they attributed Ronald Reagan's success entirely to voters designated "pro-family" or "pro-moral." State NRPR leaders involved in the races in question, however, were far more cautious in their claims.

A factor we find significant is the tendency of NRPR-backed winners to play down the effect of the religious vote. We can only draw the conclusion that a significant number of these victorious candidates would like not to be identified too closely with the NRPR. During the campaign, some candidates attempted to keep the NRPR at a distance, while at the same time enjoying the benefits of its presence. Some who duplicated CV-provided Congressional report cards at their own expense deny any substantial involvement with the NRPR. Clearly, some pragmatic politics is being played here. If the NRPR intends to be active anyway, there is not much point in telling its people to go back to their pews. But just in case the NRPR goes too far, attacks one's opponent unfairly or too stridently and causes a backlash, it is best not to be perceived as the NRPR candidate. We think it is safe to say that most candidates welcome NRPR support as long as they are able to keep it at a safe distance. The result is that incumbents targeted for defeat are forced to fight two enemies—the Republican (in virtually all cases) challenger and the NRPR. In races where combined forces of MM, CV, NCPAC, and CSFC are active, the enemies multiply.

In many cases, the negative advertising employed in the 1980 elections by the New Right in general was intentionally "low-road," so that the favored candidate might "take the high road," in the words of one New Right leader. Mere association with an issue unpalatable to significant portions of the population may very well damage a person's political image, regardless of his or her position on the issue. The extensive use of independent campaigns run by political action committees allowed elections to become virtual street brawls, with only one candidate becoming bruised. While one opponent was locked in a distasteful battle with the PACs, the other could go about the business of campaigning in a dignified "Congressional" manner.

One NRPR version of this strategy took place in the Iowa senatorial race in which John Culver felt so unfairly attacked by the NRPR that he imported the pastor of his Maryland church to attest to his Christian credentials. During televised debates, Culver made the mistake of criticizing his opponent's campaign for injecting religious issues into the race. Charles Grassley, the eventual winner, actively supported by the entire NRPR, and for whom church appearances were simultaneously a religious and political activity, could accurately reply that he did not inject religion into the campaign, but that *Culver* had done so with his imported clergyman. While it probably is true that Grassley had not injected religion into the campaign as an issue, it may be primarily a technical truth. It is also true that Grassley did not need to inject religion into the campaign—the NRPR had injected it for him. Some organized religiously based opposition did emerge in Culver's favor, as well as some fear of backlash, but Grassley clearly benefited. One question raised by this episode, which both candidates seem to have found uncomfortable, concerns the moral and political responsibilities of a candidate who is likely to benefit from PAC activity, but who finds that activity objectionable. We will return to this issue in the last chapter.

Occasionally we found people who had been elected with NRPR support who were rather reluctant to talk with us. More than once we were asked, This isn't going to get us in trouble, is it? One congressman would not allow us to speak with his staff unless his press secretary were also present. (Press secretaries are experts at not answering questions and keeping everyone happy, except perhaps the questioner.) We interpret this reticence as an indication of the influence of the NRPR. People in Congress believe that they can be hurt politically both by the NRPR and by its opponents, no matter what stands they may take on the issues involved. A major ingredient in this discomfort is the fact that no one is quite sure of the rules of the game, nor are they likely to be, for some time.

The NRPR's injection of religiously held convictions into the political process was more pronounced in 1980 than in the recent past. The nation at large—not merely those most directly involved in its political life—have yet to come to terms with the effect of this development. This question of the relation of America's various churches to the public realm has been raised afresh. When answers finally emerge, some new arrangements very well may have been created; meanwhile, we are in for a period of ambiguity and discomfort.

This may turn out to be the most significant impact made by the NRPR—far more than the election or defeat of a candidate here and there. The entire realm of the relation of religion to the republic is involved here. The problem that Americans of all religious and political persuasions have been called upon to solve has to do with the fundamental dimensions of our national life. The resolution that finally is achieved will involve input from the NRPR.

Perhaps the NRPR's most visible impact to date is the fact that it is being taken seriously. Its leading spokesmen have gained access to the nation's highest circles of power. A number of its members have attained places in government; its presence has been felt both nationally and locally. How long the NRPR will endure is difficult to say. We will return to this question, also, in the last chapter.

CHAPTER 5

Reactions from Other Religious Communities

The NRPR has drawn a considerable amount of criticism—but also some support—from a surprising array of religious communities in America. The news media, the American Civil Liberties Union, and similar groups of politicians and political analysts, both conservative and liberal, occasionally have been harshly critical. Religious bodies, including denominations and interdenominational organizations, also have called the NRPR into question, for the most part far more responsibly and insightfully than have their secular colleagues. Though Jesus promised blessing to those who are reviled for his sake (or for the sake of his cause), no one particularly enjoys being the object of criticism, still less the object of ridicule. And the NRPR has been the target of both.

The NRPR's response to its critics shows that it prefers ridicule to criticism, even though it is incensed by it. Having lived on the fringes of the culture for so long and having endured its too-often smarmy condescension, the religious "soul" of the NRPR has learned how to parry ridicule and respond in kind. Hard-shell Baptistism always has involved more than dogma.

"They're all Hitlers," a prominent film producer is quoted as saying while holding forth on the "moral majority," although we doubt that the comparison was intended to be taken literally. None of us needs to endure much of that sort of unsavory criticism before we are ready to express something stronger than righteous indignation. Patricia Harris, President Carter's Secretary of Health and Human Services, speaking at Princeton University, made the inevitible equation of the nasty turn taken by the revolution in Iran with the rise of the NRPR in the United States: "I am beginning to fear that we could have an Ayatollah Khomeini in this country, but that he will not have a beard . . . he will have a television program," Harris said.

Both the NRPR and the Islamic revolution are examples of the reassertion of traditional culture in the face of rapid social change; accordingly, one might profitably make careful comparisons. But the quotation just given is far from careful. It is safe to assume that there were hundreds of "Religion and Politics Don't Mix" editorials around the country, which conveniently ignored the fact that they have mixed—sometimes well, other times poorly— throughout American history. One leader of Moral Majority told us, "I love it when liberals accuse us of violating the separation of church and state. I say, 'What about the actions of the liberal churches in the 1960s and 1970s?'" (The secularist might conclude that both are wrong and call down a pox on both houses.) Some criticism of the NRPR was patently self-serving. *Playboy*'s "Astonishing Wrongs of the New Moral Right," by Johnny Greene (January 1981), contained some insights, but concluded, "The sterile America it would like to create would force a civil war so that [the NRPR] could extract its revenge on the public. . . . A list of censorship goals would begin with this magazine." We detect a sense of pride in this claim to be first in line at the guillotine. Jerry Falwell's congregation thoroughly enjoyed his story of the way he obtained a copy of the *Playboy* article: "I asked Don [pianist, solo vocalist, and, in this instance, straight man] to lend me his copy" (good-natured laughter). There followed a description of sending someone on the staff to buy one at the newsstand (raucous laughter). Falwell went on to tell of *Playboy*'s offer to print an interview with him. "I don't swim in sewers and I don't do interviews for pornographic magazines," had been his reply, Falwell related.[1] One month later, two European journalists claiming to be writing a book interviewed Falwell and sold the interview to *Penthouse,* a far more noxious sewer, by NRPR standards, than *Playboy.* Such unfortunate behavior did not make our task any easier. Yet one worker for the Alabama Moral Majority told us that she had read the *Penthouse* interview, found it inspirational, and was grateful that the Lord's message might thereby reach even the readers of a pornographic magazine.

The fact that the NRPR has from time to time drawn irresponsible, uncivil, and "un-American" criticism should surprise no one. It burst suddenly upon the national scene, it was abrasive from the outset, and it was, in general, not something many in the society were prepared to encounter in a constructive way. Ultimately, the NRPR really would not have preferred it otherwise. The more irresponsible one's critics, and the more they engage in ridicule instead of careful analysis, the easier they are to dismiss. The NRPR advocates at all levels have been able to counter some criticism merely with the rhetorical question, Do we lose our Constitutional rights when we become Christians?

Responses of this sort are most effective when one's critics are shallow and irresponsible. The NRPR consequently has attempted to portray all its critics as though they were saying only, You have no right to try to influence public policy. Such portrayals are self-serving, setting up straw men which can be knocked down with righteous disdain. The NRPR would like to pretend that the examples we have cited exhaust the criticism it has received. That, of course, would release it from responsibility for engaging its critics in serious discussions of substantive matters.

Our reading of the NRPR's critics, however, has demonstrated that there is a wide discrepancy between what those critics said and what the NRPR would like them to have said. The NRPR has relied on accusations of liberal smear campaigns far more than is warranted. This is not to say that there have not been some liberal smears. We find comparisons of one's opponents to Nazis particularly reprehensible, but we must point out that this particular tactic has been carried out more often by the NRPR than by its opponents. Tim LaHaye's description of Hitler's Third Reich as a "humanist" dictatorship *(Battle for the Mind)* should illustrate our point. We object to these innuendos from both sides, for two reasons. First, they distort. The pro-life advocate who equates abortion with the Nazi extermination program would have a case only if our government decided that all Roman Catholic women in the United States would be required to have abortions. The Left similarly misused the Nazi comparison in castigating American policy during the war in Vietnam; they would have had a case only if the United States had accepted the surrender of North Vietnam and then proceeded to exterminate a defenseless population. Second, the current invocations of the specter of Nazi Germany trivialize the Holocaust. To suggest that the European Jewish community was the victim of nothing more than arrogant humanism or zealous Fundamentalism is to dishonor it. To be sure, the Holocaust must stand as a disquieting reminder of man's inhumanity to man, but precisely because of the massiveness of the suffering involved, the memory of those who perished should be treated with the same respect traditionally given the sacred. Thoughtless comparisons between the United States and the Nazi regime finally serve no one and dishonor all.

Contrary to NRPR claims, its religious critics have strongly affirmed its right, as well as the right of all religious people, to enter the political arena in an attempt to influence it. "Christian Theological Observations on the Religious Right Movement," a joint statement evolving out of a meeting of leaders of fifteen major denominational bodies (Washington, D.C. [October 20, 1980]) is evidence of the mainline's good faith on this point.

> We want to register our agreement with some things we hear these companions in the U.S. Christian community saying. We agree that:
> —Christians ought to be actively engaged in politics and influenced in their political judgment by their faith in God and loyalty to God's cause.
> —Church bodies and other groups of Christians have both the right and the responsibility to make their views known on public policy issues.
> Religious leaders have both the right and responsibility to proclaim the Word of God as they understand it in light of political realities and to interpret political realities in light of the Word of God.
> —It is proper for religious bodies or organizations to provide their members and the general public with analyses of political issues and information on the voting records of office holders, and to mobilize

their members in support of or in opposition to particular legislation. We express these agreements because many criticisms of the religious right reflect what we judge to be misunderstanding of the role of the Christian community in the common life and the meaning of the constitutional principle of separation of church and state. Christians and Christian groups—whether they be ideologically on the right, the left, or in center—have every right to seek to influence public affairs.

This statement is typical of those made by moderate and liberal religious organizations throughout the United States. Jews, Baptists, Lutherans, Episcopalians, other denominational groups, and a variety of religious publications which called the NRPR into question also affirmed its right to participate in the political realm. In some cases the NRPR was taken as a reminder that Christians have a responsibility, *as Christians,* to participate in the shaping and evaluation of public policy. The Episcopal Church's House of Bishops charged that "withdrawal from political responsibility is faithless and immoral." Their pastoral letter continues: "To fail to vote or to be uninformed in voting is a denial of the biblical faith that Jesus Christ is Lord: the Lord of politics, economics, education, and social systems, as well as our personal and family lives."[2] The mainline denominations have no real quarrel with Jerry Falwell's claim that a minister is responsible "to get folks saved, baptized, and registered to vote."

The fact of NRPR politics was not the target of mainline criticism. It was the style of involvement—the methods employed, the arguments offered—to which it objected. The objections were not aimed exclusively at the religious Right and did not exempt liberals from adverse judgments. Peter Berger, writing in the *Christian Century,* condemned extremes on both sides:

If it is wrong to sanctify Americanism in Christian terms, how about the virulent *anti-*Americanism that permeates Christian church agencies and seminaries? Why is flag *waving* objectionable, while flag *burning* was an admirable expression of the prophetic mission of the church. After all, what is prophecy to one is a reprehensible misuse of Christian symbols to another. And the specificity with which the political implications of Christian faith are spelled out on the right can be matched, *pronunciamento* by *pronunciamento,* on the left.[3]

The guilt of the Left does not absolve the NRPR of responsibility to abide by the rules of political discourse. The complaint "Look at what the liberals did" can serve as well for the perpetuation of error as it can for the attainment of balance. Supporters of the Left occasionally have defended the liberal mix of religion and politics on two grounds: (a) that the Left's issues—social justice, war and peace—represent the deeper concerns of the gospel; (b) that the Left's issues were argued in the public arena on the basis of widely held secular, social, and political values, not on the basis of special revelation. Whether or not one agrees with this assessment, the two points of contrast—one theological/ecclesiastical and the other political—will serve us well in imposing some order upon denominational critiques of the NRPR and in discovering prevalent themes therein.

Mainline and Evangelical denominations were understandably offended by the NRPR's claim, acted out in the various report cards, that it held *the* Christian position on complex ambiguous issues. The notion that there might be a single legitimate Christian position on abortion struck the denominations as erroneous and somewhat dangerous. *The* Christian position on the Panama Canal or on the B–1 bomber struck them as absurd. The Lutheran Council in the U.S.A., representing the LCA, the ALC, and the Association of Evangelical Lutheran Churches, argued, "It is arrogant to assert that one's position on a political issue is 'Christian' and that all others are 'un-Christian,' 'immoral,' or 'sinful.' There is no Christian position; there are Christians who hold positions."[4] The Episcopal Church concurred with the Lutherans: "It is to be expected that we will disagree on candidates and political direction. Disagreement expresses both our freedom and the ambiguity of all choices made by sinful people in a fallen world."[5] Many Christians voice their unease that the way the NRPR presented its Christian voters' moral indexes attacked the faith of those who held differing opinions on social, economic, and political issues. Peter Berger has expressed the misgiving that the NRPR tends to exclude its political opponents from the Body of Christ:

If one says of a particular political position that it and no other is the will of God, one is implicitly excommunicating those who disagree. . . . If one believes that it is indeed God who wills the building of the MX missile, or the passage of the Equal Rights Amendment, or any specific political purpose, then one cannot remain in communion with those who reject this view and thereby posit themselves in open rebellion against God. The formula, "Thus saith the Lord" always implies the correlate, "Anathema be the one who denies this."[6]

Berger's argument does not represent only the liberal position. His concern is that membership in the Body of Christ be allowed a wide variety of political persuasions, lest Christ's transcendence over the world be collapsed and Christ be imprisoned in humanly contrived programs. *Sojourners,* an Evangelical publication which seeks to apply biblical faith to social issues, argued much the same point in a series of articles on "God and Caesar":

In both the New and Old Testaments, God and his kingdom are viewed as the only objects of ultimate authority and loyalty. If the state presumes to demand such allegiance, it must be politely ignored. In the New Testament, the specifically new element is that the people of God transcend national boundaries. . . . Ultimate loyalty is to Christ and his kingdom. . . . The citizenship (to use Paul's term) of the Christian is in heaven, "the kingdom of God."[7]

There is widespread apprehension within the Christian community that their conservative brethren are too eagerly baptizing right-wing politics without regard for the whole Christian revelation or for Christianity's claim to depend on transcendent truth. The *Christian Century* proposed: "The idea that the principles of God's revelation can be neatly subsumed under the rubric of a humanly devised ideology is pretentious."[8] *Christianity Today* was less direct in tone, but no less adamant in opposing the NRPR's assertions that Christianity and liberalism are mutually exclusive. "We insist that it is possible for an Evangelical who believes in the inerrant authority of scripture to be a political moderate, or even a liberal."[9] Evangelicals, as represented by *Sojourners* and *Christianity Today,* find themselves divided between agreement with the Republicans and the NRPR on questions of individual morality, and with the liberals, Democrats, and blacks on questions of social justice. It is an interesting and potentially creative spot to occupy.

Those denominations that traditionally adhere closely to the Bible, particularly Evangelicals and Lutherans, have taken the NRPR to task for misuse of and faithlessness toward the biblical revelation. Turning the tables on the usual alignment of positions, Charles Bergstrom of the Lutheran Church in America claimed that the NRPR was *too liberal* in its use of Scripture.

> Though [NRPR groups] take pride in calling themselves "conserva-tive," much of their leadership comes from preachers with "liberal" and individualistic views of church-state relations. They often equate Christian faith with political positions on specific issues. As Lutherans we cannot accept these views.
>   The word "liberal" as I have used it here means straining Scripture to mandate specific positions on social justice issues. . . . It is biblically liberal to bend the word of God to fit your political ideas.[10]

Carl Henry, America's leading Evangelical thinker, expressed his concern over what Peter Berger called the "effortless linkage between reactionary religion and reactionary politics."[11] Henry shares the NRPR's concern over societal decay. He writes that "fierce moral relativity is encompassing our secular society," which has "lost its biblical moorings" and consequently is fraught with "rampant perversion of sex, the breakdown of family life, and the cruelty and inhumanity evident in the ready massacre of fetal life."[12] But Henry takes issue with the NRPR's "bullying use" of Scripture cited by the Episcopal bishops. "Evangelical churches need to speak out on both the gospel of grace and the revealed principles of social and political life," Henry claimed. "This must be done without confusing specifics valid only for the Hebrew theocracy with civic imperatives for pluralistic nations envisioned in the New Testament," he added, contradicting the assertions made by Falwell and others that only the "ceremonial" law of the Hebrew Scriptures is invalid today. In Carl Henry's view,

> The Bible gives no blueprint for a universal evangelical political order. The Moral Majority was misguided by its leaders, who

promoted a Christian litmus test of specific issues used to approve or disapprove particular candidates. Its spokesmen retreated to an espousal of "principles" without carefully defining them or logically deriving specifics from them.[13]

A *Christianity Today* editorial written less than two months before the 1980 elections argued that the NRPR's linkage of biblical models to right-wing policies constituted an illegitimate use of the Scriptures:

> The Bible isn't always explicitly clear on how its principles are to be understood and applied to every specific issue. These applications are not always divinely given in the Word of God. Our best efforts to be biblical and moral on current political, social and economic issues are still limited, very fallible human applications of the infallible Scripture. We must be prepared to recognize, therefore, that sincere and conscientious Christians may apply these principles in different and sometimes contradictory ways. Recognizing the diversity in the body of Christ, Christians must allow for these differences in application of God's truth.[14]

Both Carl Henry and Paul Moore, bishop of the Episcopal diocese of New York, have suggested that NRPR misappropriation of the Bible may be due in part to the absence of tradition, or historical consciousness, that is characteristic of NRPR groups. Henry claims that "the Evangelical right lacks historical perspective, theological depth, and philosophical rationale."[15] Bishop Moore suggests that, contrary to usual classifications, it is The Episcopal Church and similar institutions which deserve to be seen as the true conservatives. Moore notes that the church maintains Scripture, sacraments, episcopal polity, creeds, tradition, and artifacts which allow it to "rejoice in a flexible ethos," while conserving the "heart of the faith . . . a passionate love for the Lord Jesus Christ, the clear and ringing witness to the principles of redemption, justice, freedom, peace and love."[16]

The Evangelical perspective, represented by Carl Henry, and the liturgical tradition, represented by Bishop Moore, differ from the "core" churches of the NRPR in a number of respects. One difference is a sense of embeddedness in history, or a lack thereof. Henry and Moore hail from tradition—ways of corporate life in which the present is conditioned by the events and forms of the past. In important respects, those such as Jerry Falwell do not. Falwell represents yet another Protestant perspective in which the erosion and nurture of time is not felt. Leaping from the present back to the time of God Incarnate, this American tradition has proposed to establish the New Testament Church, something which, for Roman Catholic Christians, among others, can be accomplished only in the mystery of the Sacrament. Church history—indeed, the whole life of the church—must count for naught as we equate two mystical moments, the earliest church and our congregation here and now. The notion of development is heretical from this perspective, for it suggests images of growth and increased understanding—concepts now in the lexicon of Darwinian evolution. Against a static model of the New Testament Church, all development constitutes deviance.

A related criticism of the NRPR was voiced by Bishop Moore, who took note of the fact that those churches most central to the NRPR lack democratic polity. The positions supported consequently do not really represent the fruit of the labors of the community of saints. In the act of worship, for example, there is little for the congregation to do—no liturgy (the "work of the people"), no service to perform. The congregation is an audience, played to by a minister who, in turn, is prompted by God. This is one of the primary reasons American Fundamentalism adapted so easily to television. Yet one must wonder along with the traditionalists, What happens when groups of people lose their sense of historical conditioning and embeddedness? Does one forfeit the ability to learn from history; forfeit the opportunity to gain some perspective on one's current world-view? A lack of perspective on oneself and one's group may lead one to become arrogant, imperious, uninterested in debate because unwilling to listen. A pamphlet on the New Right published by The United Methodist Church catches this dimension of the NRPR:

> The "New Religious Right" has also made the same mistake committed by the social gospeler earlier in the century. They exaggerate the sins of their opponent and negate any original sin of their own. They have become victims of what Reinhold Niebuhr

called "easy conscience," or what the New Testament describes as the self-righteousness of the Pharisees.[17]

Sojourners, too, concerns itself with the implications of the rule of the righteous: "Since human power is inconsequential in the light of God's kingdom, human pretentions to power are simply games, evil games full of pride and violence. . . . 'It shall not be thus among you,'" *Sojourners* warns, "'but whoever wants to become great among you will be your servant and whosoever will be first among you, will be slave of all' (Mark 10:42-43)."[18] To balance the *Sojourners* perspective, it is necessary to add that Christianity (indeed, any religion) must come to terms with the difficulty of wielding power, if it is to remain in the world, the place of power. Otherwise Christanity will limit itself to the form of a victim's religion. To cite *Fiddler on the Roof,* "It's no disgrace to be poor, but it's no great honor, either."

Not surprisingly, it is those closest to the world-view of the NRPR who often have been its keenest critics. Carl Henry locates the arrogance of the NRPR in its confusion of the inerrancy of Scripture with the inerrancy of its own interpretation and application of Scripture. *Christianity Today* similarly admits the possibility of arriving at a biblically informed "position on Zimbabwe, or disarmament, or the Panama Canal" (all on NRPR report cards). But, it warns, "Even if we see these principles [upon which our position is based] with scintillating clarity . . . they must be applied to the present world situation."[19] For Evangelicals such as Carl Henry and *Christianity Today,* the Bible is not self-applying. For the NRPR, it is. In fact, the NRPR ultimately denies that it applies the Bible at all; it merely renders obedience to the Word of God and allows the Word to "flow through" it. This is a serious point of contention between the NRPR and other types of Evangelicals. Henry and *Christianity Today* finally charge the NRPR with denying the presence of a human element at a crucial point in its theological/political program. Throughout the history of Christianity, the treating of humanly wrought things as if they were divine has gone by the name of idolatry.

This sensitivity to the adoration of things human has prompted Evangelicals' concern that the NRPR may represent "civil religion" in the sense of national self-worship (see chapter 6). Paul D. Simmons, a professor at Southern Baptist Theological Seminary, for example, writes of the NRPR: "It amounts to a coalition of ultra-conservative religion, laissez-faire capitalism and American nationalism. The result is a fervent religious movement that could easily pass for a reactionary political movement. They are equally committed to God, Adam Smith, and George Patton—but not necessarily in that order." Simmons goes on to argue that "fundamentalist civil religion allies itself with the most fervent forms of nationalistic pride." He also notes that Fundamentalism genuinely fears "that America might be bypassed as the bearer of the torch of God among the nations of the earth."[20]

While Simmons' critique sometimes resorts to the kind of stridency that characterizes much NRPR literature, his last point seems particularly illuminating. The most disturbing aspect of civil religion, for Simmons, is the effort to manipulate God.

> America is not a *Christian Country but a country in which many Christians happen to live.* America is called of God to seek justice and serve the common good of humanity. That is not a place of special privilege, however, but a special responsibility. Civil religion is idolatrous precisely because it substitutes temporal loyalties for eternal verities. Identifying the Judeo-Christian posture with American nationalism is to lose the transcendent and absolute nature of the Christian faith. For Christians and Jews, loyalty to God must transcend any earthly loyalties.[21]

The result is further idolatry: "To decide that our enemies are God's enemies is to substitute nationalistic ideology for Christian theology." This critique of nationalistic civil religion fears that the NRPR ultimately represents an attempt to exert control over God, to impose ourselves upon God as a most beloved child, a chosen people. In a reversal of the biblical paradigm, the NRPR, in effect, proposes to redeem God, to rescue God from the dustbin of history. From the perspective of its Evangelical and mainline brothers, the NRPR is overcompensating for its lack of faith.

In its "Statement on Religion and Politics," the Lutheran Council of the U.S.A. rediscovered a timely doctrine in its heritage:

"Lutherans acknowledge the two-fold reign of God, under which Christians live simultaneously. God is the ruler of both the world and the Church. The Church is primarily the agency of the Gospel in the new age of Adam."[22] Charles Bergstrom draws out the implications of the Lutheran position in his comments on secular humanism. He writes: "What some television preachers call secular humanism is, in fact, not an evil, but a different way in which God works. Secular is not necessarily godless and use of religious terms is not always holy."[23] From the Lutheran perspective, the NRPR represents an attempt to collapse the age of Christ into the age of Adam. It claims to have plumbed the mind of God, to have received answers to highly specific political questions directly from the mouth of authority. It further claims that God has little choice as to a worldly servant; either it is the NRPR, or no one at all. It has stripped God of Mystery, a feature so predominantly present in liturgical and sacramental traditions, and in Luther's doctrine of the *deus absconditus*; it has claimed understanding perfect enough to illuminate the age of Adam. God no longer moves in mysterious ways—through the theories of Darwin and Einstein, the ineffable effects of the Eucharist, or even the prompting of the Spirit—but in ways thoroughly transparent to the mind of the NRPR. Jerry Falwell urges his congregation to memorize Scripture so that when they are confronted with a problem-ridden choice, God can cause the appropriate verse to come to mind, a doctrine of inspiration which illustrates the extent to which the Bible has replaced the Holy Spirit (and the Spirit's unpredictability) in this dimension of American Protestantism. Its Christian critics see the NRPR as attempting to interpose itself between God and the world, to limit God's access to the world, and to give the world what the NRPR believes is the only access to God—the NRPR.

We need to consider once again the magnitude of difference between the positions on biblical inerrancy held by Evangelicals such as Carl Henry and those held by the NRPR. Henry believes he possesses an inerrant text and flawed understanding, while the religious core of the NRPR claims an infallible text *and infallible understanding*. The paradox of the NRPR's comprehension of human reason is readily apparent in its condemnation of humanism on the one hand and its assumption of perfect understanding on the other. The NRPR insists upon an absolute Fall; it castigates Thomas Aquinas' understanding of reason as part of the *imago dei* as an incomplete doctrine of the Fall. For the NRPR, the *imago* must be totally obliterated; human nature must be entirely corrupt. But that is only half the story, or perhaps even less. For the NRPR, human nature is also eminently transformable. It can be born again into a state of being that knows no uncertainty and attains perfect understanding, unfettered by the weight of human finitude. We have here an either/or proposition, both ends of which are totalistic. Paul Simmons properly calls this a form of Gnosticism.[24] Ultimately, it is a religion of enlightenment, snapping its converts from total depravity to easy grace.

The Christian community's perception of arrogance on the part of the NRPR is based largely upon NRPR Gnosticism. Fidelity to its own position requires the NRPR to reject "humanist" or even "liberal" Christian critiques as mere ranting born of a fatally flawed perspective. Only those voices that speak from the realm of enlightenment deserve a hearing. It is a hermetically sealed position, deeply distrustful of dialogue, oriented to proclamation rather than to conversation. Those outside the NRPR who have expressed fears of tyranny and of the end of pluralism are reacting to the NRPR's claim to perfect enlightenment, a claim that deprives both secularists and Christians of a legitimate standpoint from which to speak in the world.

Gnosticism is akin to magic in its assumption that spiritual enlightenment and moral purity will eliminate a wide range of worldly problems. Peter Berger has issued a warning against such tendencies:

> The idea that moral sensitivity somehow bestows the competence to make policy recommendations under the sun is delusional. It is also an idea that seems to have deep roots in American Church history. . . . The consequence, repeatedly, has been what one might call inflationary prophecy. The prophet who solemnly tells the people what they ought to do may get away with this once or twice, especially if the recommendations do not lead to immediate and highly visible disaster. The prophet who keeps on doing this soon loses credibility.[25]

Carl Henry, among others, has been disturbed about the NRPR's "quick fix" attitude, which he suggests "misunderstands the depth of sinful perversity."[26] But for those who cling to notions of total regeneration, the quick fix appears a reasonable reward for purified faith. The NRPR has been faulted by many Christians, particularly Evangelicals, for its narrow focus upon issues. "Private" morality, they have noted, consumes a large portion of the NRPR's moral vision, often to the exclusion of social concerns. From the NRPR perspective, private morality—sexuality and the like—is seen to hold broad social implications: If one attains a proper private relationship with God, the world will involuntarily be transformed—"These things shall be yours as well."

The magical tendencies of the NRPR have not been lost on the *Christian Century:*

> Like the foes of alcohol, Falwell believes that America's fate hinges on adoption by government of . . . latter-day prohibitions. If we can just quash sufficient numbers of deviants and dissenters, he implies, America's problems will disappear and its former greatness will be regained. We need not worry, it seems, about the depletion of our resources, the poisoning of our environment, the onrushing arms race, or the failings of our industries.[27]

The NRPR, however, has seen no cause for alarm in its judging of public officials on a narrow range of moral issues and in its urging election or defeat on that basis. In NRPR terms, moral rectitude entails political competence. For other Christians, it does not.

Christianity Today has taken strong exception to the NRPR's attempt to convert elections into moral referenda.

> It will not do . . . to focus upon a single issue, or even two or three so-called moral issues. In today's world, not one issue, but many, are important to the welfare of our society. It is more important to secure responsible political leaders of intelligence, deep moral commitment, political wisdom, and administrative skills than those who simply vote "right" on one or two, or even fourteen favorite issues. For the good of our nation, we must exercise a broader vision.[28]

The moral-issues rating system employed by the NRPR goes astray at two crucial points, in the opinion of its Evangelical critics:

(a) It denies the possibility of more than one biblically based position; and (b) it confuses moral purity with political competence. "Too narrow a front in battling for a moral crusade, or for a truly biblical involvement in politics," *Christianity Today* warns, "could be disastrous. It could lead to the election of a moron who holds the right view on abortion."

American religious leaders of all denominations have criticized the NRPR for insufficient commitment to social concerns. For many within the Christian community, responsiveness to the needs of the poor forms the heart of the gospel. Congressman Walter E. Fauntroy, a black minister and the District of Columbia's Representative, expresses the consensus opinion:

> I take strong exception to the application . . . of religious principles to a very narrow range of secondary political issues, while blatantly opposing the application of religious principles to a broad range of primary political issues.
>
> Christian believers have a responsibility to advocate the "whole gospel." That whole gospel is caught up in our Lord's inaugural address: "The Spirit of the Lord God is upon me; because he hath anointed me to heal the broken-hearted, to preach deliverance to the captives and recovery of sight to the blind, to set at liberty them that are bruised." (Luke 4:18)[29]

The NRPR's perceived lack of commitment is seen by its Christian critics to be one of its most serious religious failings. Many have felt that the NRPR denies the legitimacy of social-welfare programs by arguing that they (a) produce lazy freeloaders, and (b) steal from the hard-working to give to the undeserving. Some were offended when Falwell dismissed the likely effects of reduced welfare upon the poor by comparing their plight to that of his dogs, who had to learn to eat dry (inexpensive) dog food. Those of Evangelical persuasion are quick to add warnings regarding the massive failure of socialism. There is now a broad-based movement within American Christianity which is striving to free the social gospel from its captivity on the Left and restore it to its roots—to a biblical faith aware of its own limitations but dedicated to the presentation of the whole gospel. To its credit, Moral Majority also has taken some halting steps in this direction. Jerry Falwell announced a much-heralded ten-point program to meet the needs of the poor. The heart of Falwell's proposal is that suburban congregations "adopt" inner-city churches and assume some responsibility for their well-being. The Reverend E. V. Hill has been assigned the task of preparing a program for social action. In the six months since the proposal was announced, *Moral Majority Report* has made infrequent mention of it. That fact, however, should not be taken as conclusive evidence that the idea was a purely symbolic gesture on the part of Moral Majority. Social action is a far more difficult and time-consuming enterprise than those that can be accomplished through direct-mail solicitations. Falwell also has employed his apparatus to benefit several relief projects. Although the money sought is meager in comparison to the amount Moral Majority and the "Old-Time Gospel Hour" could raise in concert, the effort need not prove insignificant.

In *The Public Church,* Martin Marty suggests that American Christians need to meet the NRPR on its own terms.

> Biblical literalists have to confront the texts, texts which give far more space to justice among classes of people or to the problem of poverty than to the issue of profanity or pornography. Yes, one must say to them, let us take the prophets literally, as you claim to. "It is written, and I insist . . ." is a phrase that would have great power.[30]

Except perhaps to jolt mainline denominations out of their scriptural slumber, Marty's advice may be superfluous. Already there are dedicated Evangelicals doing precisely what he suggests: They are calling upon both the NRPR and the mainline to observe the whole gospel—the good news of social justice and of redemption. They would like nothing better than to win co-workers from both Left and Right, perhaps imparting a recovery of origins to one and a powerful social conscience to the other.

Our readers should be aware that in our review of Christian criticism of the NRPR, we have sought to orchestrate somewhat disparate voices into a cogent chorus. That is one of the purposes of our effort—to uncover the various themes swirling about the

NRPR phenomenon and to allow them to be heard a little more clearly above the din. There has been relatively little anger in the Christian critiques we have read, and only occasional condescension. Almost no criticism of the "get your Christianity out of politics (while leaving mine in)" variety has turned up. Most of the critiques have availed themselves of the resources entailed by the Christian tradition, its biblical roots, and its theological and ecclesiastical heritage. Many of the critiques have posed questions of considerable importance and urgency.

The credibility of the NRPR could rest upon its willingness to listen to and engage these voices, in order to further common understanding rather than to score victories. Ten years from now, we could find that the NRPR represents but one aspect of a much larger self-reassessment and reorientation on the part of American Christianity.

America's Jews always have been concerned about right-wing politics, and they make no exception of the NRPR. Sharing relatively little common religious ground with the NRPR, Jews have expressed their criticism in the language of the American civil liberties tradition. They defend the tradition of religious pluralism and question anything that might undercut it. Some Jews, for the most part from the Orthodox sector, have supported the NRPR, owing to agreement on issues such as abortion, pornography, and aid to private education. However, these supporters do not constitute a significant percentage of the American Jewish population. Most American Jews seem extremely wary of the NRPR, while at the same time they are grateful for its support of Israel. The NRPR's militant Christianity and its equally militant pro-Israel posture have placed America's Jews in something of a quandary and have produced conflicting responses from within the Jewish community.

Jews do not believe the NRPR organizations are anti-Semitic, and yet they are concerned about the NRPR and anti-Semitism as linked issues. The divergent reactions are clearly visible in statements produced by various Jewish leaders. The November 18, 1980, *Trends Analysis Report,* published by the American Jewish Committee, states flatly:

No known anti-Semites are identified with the New Right, and the principal groups have made no public overtures to the several Klan and Nazi groups who endorse New Right positions on various issues. While the history of American populism is replete with attempts by populist leaders to scapegoat Jews, this latter-day movement is not discernibly anti-Semitic.[31]

Rabbi Alexander Schindler, president of the Union of American Hebrew Congregations, the major Reformed association, sees a different phenomenon:

I do not say that the Jerry Falwells are deliberately fomenting anti-Jewish sentiments and violence. But I do say their preachments have that inevitable effect. When ministers assert . . . that only one brand of politics has God's approval . . . intolerance takes rootage. When the Moral Majority demands a Christian Bill of Rights and a prominent churchman adds that "God almighty does not hear the prayers of Jews," there should be no surprise when synagogues are destroyed by arson and Jewish families are terrorized in their homes. . . .

Such preachments have their inevitable effect. They breed hatred for the Jew.[32]

For Jews, the issue is not whether the NRPR is anti-Semitic, but whether it: (a) fosters anti-Semitism; (b) jeopardizes America's traditions of religious pluralism; (c) promulgates an understanding of America (as a "Christian nation") which would tend to exclude Jews from full participation in the society; and (d) encourages heavy-handed evangelism, which Jews find uncivil and oppressive, and which would have as its purpose the elimination of the Jewish community through conversion.

Were it not for its position on Israel, it seems safe to say that almost all Jews would be vehemently opposed to the NRPR. However, the NRPR's staunch support of Israel has complicated the relationship between these two groups. For Rabbi Schindler, the NRPR's support of Israel has a hollow ring.

The deepest reasons for the support given to Israel by the evangelical Fundamentalists are theologically self-serving. As they read Scripture, Jesus cannot return for the Second Coming until all the Jews are in the whole of their Biblical land and then are converted to

Christianity. Only true believers can enter the gate of heaven. Devout Jews, if they refuse to accept Jesus, will not be permitted beyond those pearly gates. They will be buried beneath Mount Zion once the newer Israel replaces the old. This is their apocalyptic vision in all its fullness: they seek our extinction as a particular people. Why then in heaven's name should we give them recognition? Have we lost all self-respect? We may have to meet with them, talk to them, even deal with them. But surely we need not applaud them. When we do, it is a madness—and suicidal.[33]

One of the leaders of America's Jewish Community who has met with, talked to, and dealt with the NRPR, and who does not fear to offer some applause, is Marc Tanenbaum, director of the American Jewish Committee. In an article for *Hadassah* magazine (April 1981), Tanenbaum presents a genuinely optimistic view of American Evangelicalism. He notes that the institutionalization of religious liberty is, in no small way, attributable to Evangelicals and that when some within the NRPR "began advocating the establishment of a 'Christian America' . . . and were urging their followers to 'vote for born again Christians only,' the first Americans to oppose that Constantinian view were Southern Baptist leaders."[34] Those whom Tanenbaum is citing, however, are Evangelicals of a very different sort from those who populate the NRPR. But Tanenbaum and the NRPR see eye to eye on Israel:

> While many liberal Protestant church bureaucrats have become willing instruments for PLO politics and propaganda, the vast majority of Evangelical Christians have remained steadfast in their support of Israel as a Jewish state. . . . American Jewry would be foolish to take that for granted, and self-destructive to alienate that support by engaging in theological casuistry over why Evangelicals and Fundamentalists really support Israel. There is a wise rabbinic teaching that "even though the intention may not be pure [for the sake of heaven], the effects can be pure."[35]

In the spring of 1981, Tanenbaum and Falwell issued a joint statement, noting that each looked for the coming of the Messiah—Tanenbaum for the first time, Falwell for the second. Might that be all it takes—some good humor, and Jerry Falwell looking into his Bible to discover that waiting for the Messiah is sufficient unto salvation? Perhaps it is not unthinkable, no matter how great the degree of unlikelihood. In the same issue of *Hadassah* in which Tanenbaum's defense of Evangelicalism appeared, Arthur Hertzberg, president of the American Jewish Congress, was less optimistic. "As a Jew," Hertzberg wrote, "I am not cheered by the support for Israel expressed by some of the major figures of the New Right."[36] Hertzberg's reason was much the same as Schindler's—that NRPR support for Israel appears to be predicated on the role Israel plays in the Fundamentalists' vision of the apocalypse. Hertzberg crystalized his sense of danger: "Some Christian Zionists . . . as they wax enthusiastic about the realm of the Jews, also talk about the need, in the short run, to make the existing gentile society totally Christian. The Jews belong in the Holy Land—and not in America."

The underlying problem here is the distinction between support for Israel and respect for Judaism. Anti-Judaism is a more pertinent issue to raise with regard to the NRPR than is anti-Semitism. Throughout the history of Judaism's uneasy relationship with Christianity, the claim that has faced both communities is that Christianity has replaced Judaism in the covenant. From the Christian perspective, there has been no good reason for Judaism to continue to exist. In the Christian view, it almost invariably has been impossible to be simultaneously a Jew and in a proper (saving) relationship with God. We have no doubt that this denial of Judaism's religious integrity has severely undercut the security of Jewish communities living in Christian lands. Although Falwell argues that Israel (and hence Jews) have no better friends than American Fundamentalists, he describes the settlement of Jewish people in Israel since 1947 as the Jews' return "to the land of their unbelief."[37] Yet Falwell also believes that anyone who oppresses Israel (and hence the Jewish people generally), will feel God's wrath.

The Jewish community is correct in hearing a double message. During the course of our research, we have observed that the NRPR answers every question about anti-Semitism or Judaism with statements about Israel. It is as if the NRPR found it inconceivable that Judaism and Israel might be separate entities. Consequently, the American Jews are justifiably anxious. In our conversations with groups within local communities, we found that their most immediate and urgent concern had to do with the integrity of Judaism as a religion. Parents were distressed by the fact that many Jewish children refused to ride the schoolbuses for fear of oppressive evangelization—virtually "conversion by capture." When Jews behold the rumblings of an evangelical revival, when they hear Christians calling for the conversion of the nation, when they observe an aggressive religious/political movement to gain access to power, they can be expected to assert America's tradition of religious pluralism.

In a sense, the reason Bailey Smith's *faux pas,* "God almighty does not hear the prayer of a Jew," was most disturbing to Jews may not have been the claim to exclusive communication rights, but the fact that it was set in the political context. Protestants and Catholics have been saying similar (and often worse) things about each other for centuries. The "We're saved, you're damned" syndrome is hardly new. The innovation in Smith's Dallas statement, from the Jewish perspective, was his *introduction* to the now famous quotation: "It is interesting at great political rallies how you have a Protestant to pray, a Catholic to pray, and then you have a Jew to pray. With all due respect to those dear people, my friends, God Almighty does not hear . . ."—the question in Jewish minds is, What *is* their due respect? Does Smith suggest that Christianity should have a monopoly on the official acknowledgment of the special place of religion in the society conferred by things as prayer at political events? And if so, then what is the status of Judaism in America? The religious security of American Judaism is as much at stake as the political security of Israel.

We expect that American Jews will vigilantly guard America's religious pluralism. In so doing, they will inevitably come into conflict with the NRPR over issues involving the separation of church and state. A large majority of Jews will vigorously oppose such NRPR legislation as school prayer, which is perceived to threaten Jewish legitimacy in America. On the issue of Israel and the protection of the security of the Middle East, Jews and the NRPR seem likely to cooperate. Tanenbaum, in essence, urges Jews to reinforce what they take to be the best of the NRPR. As for the rest, particularly the status of Judaism in American society, Jews are likely to align themselves with the mainline and continue their dialogue with the Evangelicals from the *Sojourners* and *Christianity Today* camps and with the Evangelical denominations outside the NRPR. As soon as Bailey Smith's comment about unheard Jewish prayers was reported, Marc Tanenbaum was instructing reporters (correctly) that Smith's statement was "almost at total variance with the major pronouncements of the Southern Baptist Convention." We expect that Tanenbaum's attitude will prevail in American Judaism for the next few years. There will be occasional cooperation with the NRPR on limited matters and an openness to discussion, but also deep wariness and relentless opposition in a number of areas. Jews will not be alone in this posture, but will be joined by a number of Christian friends, some of them newly found.

CHAPTER 6

American Civil Religion and the NRPR

The term *civil religion* has come into public view within the past fifteen years. America's civil religion has been the subject of a slow but continually developing public discussion: What is the civil religion? Does it really exist? If it does, where? What is its relation to denominational religions? What are the social conditions that give rise to it?

In general, *civil religion* has been used to designate the coming together of the political life of a people and the transcendent dimensions of reality, integrating a nation into the life and order of the cosmos. The American civil religion, whatever it is, specifically, in its several meanings, is predicated on there being something about our public political life that points beyond itself—*above* itself, we might say—to ultimate or eternal reality. More simply stated, civil religion highlights the fact that our public political life is connected to matters weightier than Constitutions, laws, officeholders, and specified procedures. It is related also to symbols, metaphors, and values that shape our whole way of responding to the world. For these, some rather large claims are made, to the effect that there is something special about our public political life because it is rooted in reality greater than any one people and government, and because it calls us to loyalty and heavy responsibility.

Despite the rough contours of the debate over exactly what the American civil religion is, the NRPR does have something to do with it—indeed, the NRPR is quite explicitly and self-consciously attempting to call upon, identify with, and shape America's civil religion. A good part of the struggle between the NRPR and many of its opponents will certainly be over the view of the civil religion that will prevail in the society as a whole. The NRPR has consistently presented itself as concerned primarily with the spiritual/moral realm, yet it claims ultimate political consequences for this dimension of American life. The crucial issue is understood as one involving America's survival within a divinely ordered universe.

It is not a serious distortion to say that at its heart, the NRPR represents a resurgence of some traditional forms of American civil religion. In some ways, this is really nothing very new. The particular forms of civil religion espoused by the NRPR have been around for a long time; some date back to the beginnings of the colonial period and found their quintessential expression in New England Puritanism. It is our conviction that the NRPR has brought together a number of styles of civil religion—styles that have been identified by various students of the issue, but which too often have been brought forward individually as *the* American civil religion. Consequently, before proceeding further with a discussion of the NRPR and civil religion, a brief description of the current models is in order.

There are almost as many views of civil religion as there are writers on the topic, but the variety is not endless and all must work with certain basic themes. Rather than forcing a choice among various models, we believe a more sensible procedure is to grant that each view has seen something that is actually there, or at least that has been present at a particular time and so may be available for renewal. In short, what has been debated as the civil religion might better be called the civil religion *complex,* allowing for a multiplicity of forms and styles that may coexist (probably with a good deal of overlap) in different segments of the population and that may compete with one another for dominance, depending upon historical circumstances.

1. One of the more obvious but less palatable forms of civil religion is blatant chauvinism, a straightforward national self-

worship, often couched in the assumption that American society represents a level of human achievement toward which all other societies are striving. The reference to America occasionally used in President Carter's speeches to plead for national confidence and unity—"This, the greatest nation on earth"—may have struck some as empty but required ritual, but it nonetheless appealed to a cherished American notion of our place in the general order of human existence. Carter's sense of the civil religion was far more complex than this perhaps unkind example indicates, but he nevertheless joined those who tapped into a deep-seated American conviction of our significance on the world stage.

The danger of national self-worship, of course, is idolatry, a problem which Will Herberg properly identified in his now-classic *Protestant, Catholic, Jew*. Others, most notably the Niebuhr brothers, Reinhold and H. Richard, have issued the same warning. An idolatrous nation runs the risk of absolutizing its own limitations. It not only can impose its political system, technology, and culture willy-nilly around the globe, with full confidence that it is doing its victims a favor, but it also can stymie its own growth in and adaptation to the changing world around it. The nation becomes arrogant, imperious, and stultified. And it probably becomes universally disliked, as it crushes indigenous populations beneath what it assumes is the inevitability of progress and modernization.

2. But often the civil religion complex is not as simple as straightforward self-worship, despite the presence of such tendencies. Herberg noted that Americans are highly idealistic—perhaps the world's most idealistic people. Many of the ingredients he found in the civil religion, such as optimism, democracy, and individualism, were themselves ideals—not so much descriptions of what America is; as visions of what it might be or what it should strive to be.[1] This then is a second form in the civil religion complex: a commitment to and reverence for a set of ideas, a "real America" established by the founding fathers, dedicated to the recognition that all men are created equal and possess certain inalienable rights, and committed to fulfilling that dream. There is an element of judgment here that is not present in straightforward worship. We can be held accountable to Mr. Jefferson and his colleagues, and we can be found wanting.

A further dimension is present in this style of civil religion. It is creativity. Contrary to superficial readings of sociological and anthropological theories which allow religion only to reflect or reinforce a more basic social reality, religion often plays a creative role. The formulation of ideal modes of humanity, such as good Samaritans, suffering servants, or equals before the law, creates new possibilities, which otherwise might be absent, for human existence. Critics of religion too often focus upon the closing down of human options, neglecting the way religion opens up those options. For those who scoff at the power of American ideals, it is worth remembering that Martin Luther King, Jr., in the midst of the battle for the Civil Rights Act, was able to say that black people in America really wanted only their rights under the Constitution. Part of the effectiveness of King's appeal was certainly his call for America to be true to itself.

Here the function of the civil religion is to inspire, guide, and judge.[2] One would be forced to admit that the judgment is only imperfectly carried out. The ideals themselves, embedded in documents like the Constitution, are subject to reinterpretation and change. The original Constitution allowed slavery. The amended Constitution after the Civil War allowed legal segregation. More recently, the same Constitution has been held to prohibit segregation, and the book is not yet closed. As we have indicated, the agenda of the NRPR includes the attainment of recognition for its interpretation of the Constitution, and in doing so, it stands within a noble American tradition. Yet in that process, the NRPR will be called upon to come to terms with the Constitutional guarantees of equal treatment and due process, and with the Declaration's affirmation of inherent equality and inalienable rights.

Let us understand that neither of these two forms within the civil religion complex—self-worship and venerated ideals—necessarily involves a connection with the God of western religions, or any supernatural being at all. These ways of being American can be transformed into something that can properly be called religious only by their affirmation of what Clifford Geertz terms a "general order of existence," an all-encompassing "scheme of things" which ultimately makes sense and provides human beings with a significant role to play.[3] The view that a nation represents the pinnacle and hence the conclusion of human social evolution postulates something amounting to a general order of existence. These nontheistic forms of civil religion often assume that the United States occupies a place assigned to it by "history," a kind of personification of time and change that senses external will, intelligence, and purposefulness at work within the human realm.

The same dangers present in national self-worship are present here. It is just as easy, and no less harmful, to be insensitive to the values of others as to disparage their way of life; just as easy to be imperialistic with one's own values as with one's technology. Additionally, the affirmation of ideals can be substituted for the enactment of those ideals in law and policy. Most of us probably judge ourselves by what we believe ourselves to be, not by our actual accomplishments. Ultimately, liberty and justice for all is not merely a concept, but a matter of social and political condition.

3. Unlike our first two examples, a third view of America's civil religion is explicitly religious and closely associated with Jewish (particularly Hebraic) and Christian paradigms. The image of America as God's chosen nation is one of the oldest and most enduring parts of the American self-concept. The Puritans who settled Massachusetts, and who so deeply influenced our national life, understood themselves literally to be God's New Israel, inheritors of God's covenant with Abraham, Moses, and David, which was renewed in Christ. They covenanted together before God and with God to establish a holy commonwealth, a "city on a hill," a light that would lead the nations to regeneration. They saw their passage from the Old World to the New as a repetition of the Exodus, and they were as confident of God's guidance in the American wilderness as they were that God led the first Israel through Sinai.

For the Puritans, chosenness involved the mighty burden of obedience to the terms of the covenant. Although God's New Israel may have been exceptionally blessed by divine favor, from those to whom much was given, much was required. Failure to live up to the terms of the covenant would bring divine wrath down upon New England. The clergy ceaselessly warned that God would punish those who disobeyed him. Yet God's punishment never included absolute rejection; it was always tempered with mercy, always for the purpose of instruction, and always aimed at producing repentance and a return to the covenant.

The chosen-nation style of civil religion does present some problems. For one thing, because it asserts that corporate fate depends upon a pure faith, it generates extraordinary pressures for conformity. In ethical matters, Christianity traditionally has focused upon such internal states as motivation and intention. It has harbored a vision of a transformed humanity, living not under the lordship of sin, but "in Christ." These factors occasionally have made the quest for internal conformity a lively social concern. To return to the New England Puritan example, there was no such thing as an individual fate. New England was to be judged as if it were one person. All members of the political body took part in the successes and failures of any one member. All were accountable for the sins of each. Therefore to tolerate deviance was to jeopardize the commonwealth by inviting divine wrath.

The Puritan connection of one's inner being to collective fate marks the beginning of an American quest for, perhaps obsession with, purity. If things go badly for the chosen people, the most reasonable explanation is that there has been religious or spiritual failure, a violation of the terms of the covenant. The problem may lie with the society as a whole, or it may be located specifically in a few secret deviants hidden in the midst of an otherwise pure community. Failure on the part of the chosen nation is therefore an invitation to seek out those worms at the core, identify them, and eliminate them through conversion, expulsion, or execution. When implicit faith in one's national superiority is coupled with covenantal politics, the tendency to turn inward in search of blameworthy deviants is increased. Unfortunate victims produced by that search are likely to be accused of collusion with demonic external forces: Satan, in the case of the Salem witchcraft trials; communism, in the case of the Army/McCarthy hearings.

The association of internal purity with corporate fate also has strong antipolitical overtones. All problems tend to be viewed as moral problems, almost as though the world were a mere extension of human will, with no intransigent reality of its own. Does the world fail to conform to your desires? Then look inward and cleanse the pollution from your inner parts or, alternatively, evaluate only the moral status of candidates for political office, ignoring the question of their competence. Americans have displayed a tendency to change political leaders the way one changes batteries in a flashlight. Always the hunger is for persons sufficiently pure that their goodness will chase away darkness like the dawn. Consequently, America is a nation in which inexperience can be perceived as a unique qualification for public office.

This third example in the civil religion complex is another two-edged sword. It can serve as a creative force in the society, particularly in its affirmation of social responsibilities under the covenant and in its standing in judgment on tendencies toward self-worship. Yet it also makes it possible for one to claim a divine mandate for whatever one does; to assume that since we are God's nation, our desires are God's desires. The extermination of the American Indians was rather universally justified by appealing to God's will. The very fact that European settlers, armed with guns, almost invariably defeated their Indian antagonists was itself taken to be a sign of divine approval. If God disapproved, he certainly would not have granted us victory.

4. A military conflict with another culture gave rise to an essay that initiated the entire civil religion discussion. In 1967, against the background of the Vietnam war, Robert Bellah wrote "Civil Religion in America." In that essay, he claimed that the civil religion should properly be viewed as "a genuine apprehension of universal and transcendent religious reality as seen in, or . . . revealed through the experience of the American people."[4]

Bellah was not claiming chosen-nation status for the United States, but submitting American activity to be judged by the demands of a higher order of things. The higher order that Bellah saw at the heart of America's civil religion was essentially the God and moral order of mainline Protestantism. Its central values were compassion, humility, and a high appreciation of human endeavor, coupled with a sense of the relativity of all things human.

The latter part of Ballah's essay identified what he called the "third time of trial" for the civil religion (the Revolutionary and Civil wars were the first two trials). In the third, the problem confronting America was the reconciliation of its self-understanding with a revolutionary world. There is a paradox in John Winthrop's 1630 vision of the "city upon a hill": To the extent that America serves as an example to the world, it undercuts its own centrality in world leadership. In order for other nations to follow the American example, it would be necessary for them to seek independence, control their own resources, and ultimately achieve autonomy. Our example to the world finally conflicts with our attempts to manipulate the world to our own liking.

When Bellah wrote "Civil Religion in America," his liberal audience was disposed to anything but a religious affirmation of the nation. On the contrary, the period from 1965 through Watergate saw the Left lose contact with the symbols of American nationhood. In a kind of parody of Bellah's critical civil religion, antiwar activists prided themselves on announcing that America was the most immoral nation on the face of the earth, perhaps never considering the fact that the restraint with which the war was waged was itself an indication of the government's sense of deep moral ambiguity. The Left cornered the market on prophetic moralism, but it may have alienated itself from the nation in the process.

Bellah's most recent entry into the civil religion debate is a book entitled *Varieties of Civil Religion,* co-authored with Phillip Hammond. The most significant contribution of these essays to our understanding of civil religions is the well-supported argument that civil religions in general appear in societies that are pluralistic and that also have well-developed legal systems.[5] The United States harbors a vast diversity of religious, ethnic, regional, and ideological groups and gives them all an equal right to exist, practice, and seek converts and various self-interests (but not to dominate the other groups). Consequently a crucial function is served by the mechanisms that hold the various groups together. The legal system which adjudicates disputes between equal groups is certainly one such mechanism. The other branches of government play similar roles, and the public school system is a third unification mechanism. Seen in this context, the function of the civil religion is to give legitimacy to those dimensions of public life which allow rather different groups to coexist and cooperate in the building of a national life. Without such mechanisms acknowledged by all to be legitimate, the society risks degeneration into tribal warfare. It is that warfare which may now be upon us. The Vietnam era eroded the Left's respect for national life in general, and the government in particular. The critique of national policies currently being leveled by the NRPR undercuts the legitimacy of America's public order in the same manner, but offers a replacement wearing the mantle of "true Americanism."

The NRPR clearly displays the first three styles of the civil religion complex we have identified, and an inwardly focused version of the fourth. It values America highly, selectively affirms American ideals, borrows heavily from the Puritan image of the chosen nation, and is certainly, if narrowly, prophetic. God's people are being shown their sins, warned of impending doom, and called back to faithfulness to the covenant. Unlike its Puritan predecessor, the NRPR "Jeremiad" is not spoken from the center of the culture but, in a sense, from outside it. The NRPR, consequently, must attempt to establish itself at the center. It does this in several ways.

First, there is the traditional image of America as a chosen nation. Surprisingly to some, the NRPR offers an occasional disclaimer on the matter of American chosenness. Jerry Falwell, for example, has said that he does not believe that God loves America more than he loves other nations, nor does Falwell want to wrap the cross in the flag. Yet the clear consensus among leaders of the NRPR is that America enjoys a unique relationship with God and has a special role to play in God's design for world evangelization. Falwell argues that since America has more "God-fearers" per capita than any other nation in the world, it is the only logical base for such action.[6] He also warns that evil forces will seek to destroy America precisely because she is the headquarters for Christian missions, thus tending to equate national enemies with God's enemies. For the NRPR, the mantle of the chosen people falls not upon America, but upon one section of America, a saving remnant whose presence and purity of faith may be the only reason God tolerates the rest of the nation. The NRPR quite naturally associates national survival with an explicitly Christian revival. Charles Stanley, a member of the board of directors of Moral Majority, a director of IN TOUCH Ministries, and pastor of the First Baptist Church in Atlanta writes that although one should not advocate revival just to save the

United States, it is nevertheless true that wherever there are enough Bible-believing Christians in a society, God will spare it.[7] Others are even more forthright in the association of national survival and revival. Falwell, for example, writes,

> God will again bless us if we turn back to him as individuals and as a nation. There is power in the name of Jesus Christ, and it is the only power that can turn back godless communism. If God is on our side, no matter how militarily superior the Soviet Union is, they could never touch us. God would miraculously protect America. The destiny of America awaits our choice as to what we will do with God.[8]

A second dimension of the NRPR's attempt to establish itself at the center of American culture is expressed in its official "Christian history" of the United States. Conservative Christian educational foundations, for some time, have been producing material bearing such titles as *The Christian History of the Constitution, Christian Self-Government,* and *One Nation Under God.* The purpose of this material is to demonstrate an explicitly Christian identity for the American enterprise. Once that identity is established, the NRPR can claim to be the only legitimate inheritor of the original, and hence normative, American vision. In this context, for example, Tim LaHaye writes that the time is coming when "the real American People will regain their country and culture."[9] Thus it is that the NRPR represents itself as the true America, defending the nation from those who have led us away from our original calling and have sorely tried God's patience in so doing.

The literature of the NRPR presents a fairly standardized version of American history. (Incidentally, that history appears throughout the literature—some books are dedicated entirely to the subject, and most others contain chapters or at least a series of paragraphs which condense the essentials.) The literature is all written from the perspective that American origins contain the basic models of what we are called to be and that those early models establish the parameters within which we are permitted to work. The origins of America are attributed the same kind of normative authority as the New Testament Church. As it was in the beginning, so it must be now, or else we have failed in our responsibilities as American citizens. Much of the literature consequently takes on the shape of a catalogue aimed at demonstrating the Christian identity of principal actors in the American drama.

The flow of American history is described by the NRPR as a series of alternately high and low points. The Puritans provided the first high, but their godly accomplishments did not endure and were replaced by a long period of backsliding, which was brought to a halt by the Great Awakening and the American Revolution. This second high point was again replaced by backsliding, which bottomed out in the Civil War. (The punctuation of the antebellum era by revivals defies neat categorization.) Revivals after the Civil War provided another high, followed again by a descent into the darkness of the Roaring Twenties. The period of the 1980s represents another high point. Much of the literature omits American history that occurred between the Constitution and the present, except to castigate what are taken to be negative developments. The sectioning of American history in general shows a desire to discern patterns of order from an evangelistic/revivalistic perspective. There may well be a connection here with the tradition of dispensationalism present in America, which casts all history into coherent periods.

Throughout the process of rising and falling, the key causal agent is always held to be America's faithfulness to biblical law, or morality. Spokespeople for the NRPR generally agree that God has richly blessed the United States. For Charles Stanley, God "has loved America unlike he has loved any nation of the world."[10] But a point to be recognized here is that God's blessing is not a result of God's unconditional election, or even of God's free grace. The blessing must be earned. Falwell writes: "God has blessed this nation because in its early days she sought to honor God and the Bible, the inerrant word of the living God. . . . Our great nation was founded by Godly men upon Godly principles to be a Christian nation."[11] The argument is reminiscent of rabbinical commentators who speculated that God's selection of Israel (at Sinai) could be attributed to the faith of the Patriarchs Abraham, Isaac, and Jacob.

The American Revolution and the two great documents of that period, the Declaration of Independence and the Constitution, quite naturally serve as a central focus for NRPR civil religion. Here, of course, is the moment of birth, replete with its heroes and mythic struggles for which the Puritan era serves as a prolegomenon. It is as if the seedling planted by the Puritans and watered by the Great Awakening burst forth in full bloom in 1776. Like many before them, members of the NRPR see the hand of divine providence at work in the Revolutionary period. The war was directed and ultimately won by God for the purpose of bringing the United States into being. Similarly guided were the Declaration of Independence and the Constitution, documents which have achieved almost the status of holy writ for the NRPR. They are not mere human creations, but bear the unmistakable signs of divine inspiration. The two are read as one document, the Declaration's explicit references to the Creator compensating for the absence of such references in the Constitution; the former becomes the spirit of the latter. So close is the linkage that Falwell at one point mistakenly attributes to the Constitution the phrase "and they are endowed by their Creator with certain inalienable rights."[12] From the NRPR's perspective, however, that is an error in only the most literal sense.

That the thirteen colonies could defeat Great Britain, often described as "the world's greatest military power," is itself taken as evidence of the providential nature of the Revolution. The leaders of the Continental forces, and later of the new nation, are admired both for their success and for their presumed piety. Quotations from Washington, Jefferson, Franklin, Adams, Madison, and others are assembled to demonstrate that the founding fathers held religion in high regard. The usual content of the quotations is that public order is unthinkable without religion, that the nation owes thanks to God, or that God has smiled upon American undertakings. This collection of quotations is often accompanied by accounts of the unfortunate fates suffered by the signers of the Declaration and by lists of religious phrases inscribed into the architecture of national shrines—the Washington Monument, the Supreme Court building, the Capitol rotunda, the Senate, the Library of Congress, and others. The motto In God We Trust, imprinted on American currency and postage stamps, and the words "one nation under God," from the pledge of allegiance, receive frequent mention. The effort is to show, as Donald Howard writes, that "our history is bathed in biblical references . . . [and] our culture is permeated with Biblical principles."[13] We are, in short, a Christian nation. Historical accuracy is not always the strong point of NRPR writers. The actual complexity of the founding fathers and their congenial Deism do not appear in NRPR accounts. But that is nothing new. The Revolutionary era is one which must bear the weight of legitimating virtually all those who would speak with the voice of the "true" America. As Martin Marty has noted,

> Within a generation after the national founding, Protestant America underwent particular revivals that issued in competitive churches. Almost all of the churchgoers challenged the Deist content of the Founders' faith. The rest pretended it away by converting these Founders posthumously to orthodox Christianity. Even Fundamentalists who would today reject Washington, Franklin and Jefferson from their churches as dangerous Unitarians, tend to endorse them after two centuries and claim that as Christians these were founding a privileged Christian republic.[14]

Nonetheless, the NRPR has touched a deep nerve in the American mythology, has presented that sensitive area as the original, essential America, and has identified itself as that area's only true representative. Criticism from more accomplished historians probably will not deter the NRPR in this endeavor. First of all, such criticism will be seen as yet another example of humanist thinking and dismissed as inherently biased and anti-Christian. Second, it is probably enough for the NRPR that the founding fathers be only positively disposed to religion and hence to Christianity. For some in the NRPR, even a little Christianity can go a long way. Donald Howard, for example, writes: "Even a less than totally orthodox religion based in part on the Bible, produces a higher charactered people than a religion founded wholly on the ideas of man. Mormonism, for instance, generally produces a higher charactered people than Zen Buddhism."[15]

While neither Mormons nor Zen Buddhists are likely to be pleased by this ascription, the essential message is that national success depends upon recognition of and obedience to biblical authority. Not all spokespeople for the NRPR expect school prayer to be a deeply significant spiritual experience for children.

For many, it is enough that there be simply some institutionalized recognition that there is a transcendent authority. The NRPR would, of course, prefer an explicitly Christian authority, but in a pinch, for instance in a school district with a large Islamic majority, any transcendent authority will do.

Currently, the NRPR has taken upon itself the task of condemning national sin and calling the nation back to faithfulness to the national covenant—namely, the NRPR's understanding of biblical values. As Senator Helms puts it, "Spiritually, we know we are all Israel, for Christ teaches that God's admonitions and promises to Israel will be fulfilled also in New Testament times and peoples."[16]

Consequently, what is written and said by the NRPR often takes the form of the Puritan "Jeremiad." For example, in 1691, Joshua Scottow declared:

> What is become of the primitive zeal, piety, and holy heart found in our parents? . . . Who is there left among you that saw these churches in their first glory, and how do you see them now? Are they not, in your eyes, in comparison thereof, as nothing? How is the Gold become dim?[17]

In 1980, Jerry Falwell wrote:

> It is time for America to come back to the faith of our fathers, to the Bible of our fathers, and to the Biblical principles that our fathers used as a premise for this nation's establishment. We must come back lovingly but firmly, and establish as our priorities once again those priorities that are God's priorities. Only then will we become important to God and only then will we once again know the great blessings of the power that has made and preserved us a nation.[18]

One significant difference between these two Jeremiads, separated by three centuries, is that in 1980 there was indeed more cause for complaint. The NRPR sees what it believes are a host of national sins. Behind it all, however, lies national infidelity, an intentional rejection of the founding fathers' God of the Bible by a nation gone a-whoring after other gods. The warning goes out: The sins must be recognized and repentance offered, or the nation will surely taste of God's wrath. Yet God has not rejected us. His wrath only shows that he is disappointed in his love for us. Jerry Falwell accordingly writes, "God is waiting for Americans to return to him so he can give America spiritual rebirth."[19] Spiritual rebirth, in the vision of the NRPR, will be accompanied by general success.

Let us review the styles of civil religion, noting where and how the NRPR fits into the specific variations. First, the NRPR displays some tendencies toward national self-worship. One of its more common and widely dispersed complaints is simply that the United States is no longer "number one," as if the world were one Big 10 Conference. The connection between material success and divine favor is rather easily drawn, despite the warnings from Ecclesiastes that the *wicked* often prosper. Donald Howard, for example, finds God's blessing in the productivity of free enterprise:

> Free enterprise is the greatest system of government the world has known. . . . The free enterprise system put the first man on the moon, built five times as much highway as any other nation for Americans to drive six times as many cars. It has built hospitals, supermarkets, public transportation, put two cars in most garages and made it possible for the average citizen to own his own house and fly commercial airlines.[20]

Given our current energy problems, the more ecologically minded Evangelical might wonder whether the automobile is a blessing from God or a temptation from Satan. Nevertheless, American capitalism is not only endorsed by the NRPR, but accorded divine authority. Falwell writes that "the free-enterprise system is clearly outlined in the book of Proverbs in the Bible."[21] The same claim is put forth by numerous other NRPR writers, who, alas, never cite specific chapter and verse (as is the case with other biblical endorsements). Specific proof-texts often cited in economic matters are God's "curse" in Genesis, "In the sweat of your brow you shall eat bread"—with the emphasis on *your* brow (capitalism) as opposed to someone *else's* brow (the welfare state); and II Thessalonians 3:10, "If any would not work, neither should he eat." The NRPR, of course, ignores Acts 4:32 (RSV): "Now the company of those who believed . . . had everything in common," which the Christian Left might cite as a biblical endorsement of socialism.

Regarding the second type of civil religion—acknowledgment of American ideals—the NRPR has developed a long list indeed. Occupying central positions are virtues such as patriotism, individual initiative, free enterprise, hard work, "biblical morality," respect for authority, and order. Self-reliance and local autonomy should also be included, provided one bears in mind that for the NRPR, all are dependent upon and subject to God. Democracy does not really make the NRPR's list, for it has been equated with chaos and tyranny. *Rule by law* is the preferred term, since it is more amenable to the NRPR's goal of rule by biblical law. Also generally absent from NRPR value lists is an explicit endorsement of equality. Perhaps the specters of liberation movements loom rather large here. When pushed, of course, the NRPR will affirm equality; indeed, part of its complaint is that it has been denied equality by a liberal culture. Nevertheless, up until the spring of 1981, each time the NRPR has cited "We hold these Truths to be self-evident: that all men are created equal and that they are endowed by their creator with certain inalienable rights," it has done so not to rededicate us to the pursuit of equality, but to proclaim the authority of God over our enterprises. We should also point out that the NRPR is aware of this issue and is sensitive to this kind of criticism, realizing that it is under scrutiny and that it will be judged.

The chosen-people style is very prominent in NRPR civil religion, the chief variation being that the chosen people are now a kind of nation within the nation—the "real" Americans. Yet the nation as a whole still bears the responsibility of the chosen people—obedience to God's law as revealed in the Bible. A thorough Christianizing of the civil religion takes place here, despite the NRPR's attempts to appeal more broadly. Calls for a return to biblical morality may initially seem to cut across denominational lines. However, such calls are predicated upon a reading of the Bible specific to Protestant Fundamentalism.

The civil religion of the NRPR is also deeply prophetic, at least in the sense of being critical. The criticism, however, has largely been turned inward into the arenas of faith, personal morality, and laissez faire capitalism versus the welfare state. Concerning America's position in world affairs, the NRPR civil religion is thoroughly assertive. It calls upon America to become more aggressive in pursuing its self-interest in the world and, vigorously opposing communism, to seek ultimate victory. Détente is viewed as cowardice, or worse, as treason. This is diametrically opposed to Bellah's ideal civil religion, which called upon America to reconcile itself to a Third World come of age.

The NRPR may be the very incarnation of a renewed, reformulated civil religion. It does not merely espouse civil religion—it *is* civil religion. It has stepped into the vacuum created by the Left's rejection of the symbols of America. Its version of the civil religion is probably too narrowly Fundamentalist/Protestant, too authoritarian, and too reflective of the agenda of the nonreligious Right to gain wide acceptance. Yet as Americans find their position in the world growing more vulnerable, and as the unlimited supply of cheap resources and energy force us to live more closely, the need for Americans to represent themselves to themselves for the purpose of producing a common legitimated basis for joint action should increase. Historically, civil religion has been most present and active in times of national stress, particularly war. Anything that increases the national self-consciousness, our awareness of ourselves as Americans, will also tend to bring the civil religion, in one or another of its forms, to the forefront. It would not surprise us to see the gradual development of a revitalized civil religion, more broadly drawn and less specifically Christian than that of the NRPR, but sharing a number of its concerns. It will be a consensus civil religion, affirming a vision of normative Americanism, which places collective security above individual freedoms. It will be formed in response to two of the nation's needs: the need to legitimate those mechanisms which will integrate a pluralistic society and the need to act in the world from a perspective of enlightened self-interest.

CHAPTER 7

Why Now?

No book on the New Religious/Political Right would be complete without a "why now" chapter, and no aspect of the topic is more dangerous to approach than: Why did this happen when it did? The danger lies primarily in the temptation to explain things by explaining them away. To understand anything in its historical context is to embed that thing in surrounding and antecedent processes and, to some extent, render it predictable. Explaining a thing *away* involves seeing that thing as nothing more than a product of deeper causes, denying it any life or integrity of its own, and essentially reducing it to the status of an epiphenomenon *(a by-product of prior phenomena)*. The trick, then, is to see the phenomenon in question in all its embeddedness without rendering it a mere product of forces assumed to be more real. The role of human freedom, creativity, and ingenuity must be acknowledged, along with the more usual impersonal causes.

To understand why the NRPR has emerged when it has, we should start with its justification for its own existence—the case it makes for itself. The claim the NRPR most often makes for itself is that it is engaged in turning back the tides of political, social, and moral decay. Viewed from a distance, its list of issues displays a common thread throughout: There is a sense that sacred boundaries have been violated, that things are out of place. For the NRPR, both feminism and homosexuality involve a disloca- tion of proper sexual identity. Promiscuity also is sexuality out of place—namely, outside the boundaries of marriage. Pornography involves a displacement of sex, from its proper location in the private realm into the public areas represented by television, movies, books, and magazines. Sex education in the schools is similarly out of place. Welfare represents a dislocation of proper state power, as does state interference in the educational process in general.

To our mind, the overwhelming concern of the NRPR is the question of order. The question has been stated by the NRPR itself in the starkest possible terms. There is only the choice, as the NRPR sees it, between authoritarianism and chaos. Conse- quently, those groups the NRPR has singled out as enemies are invariably described only by their most extreme representatives. The NRPR prefers its humanists to be atheists, its feminists to be lesbians, its liberals to be communists. This extreme characteriza- tion of rival positions is certainly distorting, sometimes irrespon- sibly so, but it does have the virtue of rendering choices clear, clean, and concise. The NRPR sees the world in black and white. Its doing so seems to us to be a matter of choice as much as an unconscious tendency.

To some extent, the NRPR's dichotomizing of things into stark opposites maintains the dualistic mentality of traditional Ameri- can Fundamentalism, in which all human problems are ultimately assimilated into the great conflict between good and evil, God and Satan. At another level, the NRPR's division of the world (pro-God vs. anti-God, pro-family vs. anti-family, etc.) keeps it on center stage, giving it a Messianic role. Additionally, such a division reduces the necessity for engagement and dialogue, freeing the NRPR from the politics of negotiation and compro- mise, while simultaneously launching it into the politics of lobbying and electioneering. Finally, attributing extreme posi- tions to one's opponents nudges the opponents out. Of course, this game has been played by Left as well as Right. Nevertheless, it has characterized virtually every area of conflict in which NRPR spokesmen have been engaged.

A second pervasive concern of the NRPR focuses around something we might call purity. It is strongly reflected in the extent to which images of invasion and pollution dominate NRPR literature. The United States is perceived as living in a hostile world—parasitic, ungrateful, dangerously aggressive. One writer sees us surrounded, identifying Trudeau (and hence Canada) as Marxist and also finding too much Marxist literature in Mexico for comfort. Internally, the American people are seen as being polluted by a small but powerful cadre of secular humanists who are actively conspiring against Christianity and the United States. Their venom is seeping into the school systems, the liberal churches, the labor unions, the courts, and virtually every level of the federal bureaucracy. Pornography is described in metaphors drawn from the world of infectious disease and relies on terms conveying pictures of wounds and pus, bodily invasions by agents of death. Donald Howard expresses it vividly in this story about watching the Super Bowl:

> Then the beer commercial came on. I got a sick feeling. Mrs. Howard scurried the kids on out of the room. There was that nauseating ring through our sanctified home. . . . Much less am I going to bring that dirty slimy thing [TV] into the living room and set it there with maggots crawling in it and let the stench off in my living room to pollute the nostrils of my children.[1]

Throughout NRPR literature, one repeatedly returns to images of disease. Homes, schools, the nation itself is being invaded. The social body is held to be sick. Diseased entities, principally humanists, lurk and fester within. Chaos is the fate with which they ultimately threaten us.

Thus these two aspects of the NRPR world-view—order and purity—are tightly entwined. And these sets of interrelated metaphors are so widely used by the NRPR because they make sense of experience. They identify real problems, give them a particular shape, and suggest appropriate courses of action—there is a definitive logic and rationality to the NRPR program.

Among the more interesting features of the NRPR's dichotomizing of the world is the loss of a middle ground. There is only the world of the NRPR and its opposite. One of the reasons for this, we believe, is our loss of the public world. We have already argued that the Left opted out of the civil religion during the Vietnam era, but the loss of the public world is more fundamental. If there has been a single dominant value within American culture since World War II, it has been the freedom of the individual to transact in the world with a minimum of external constraint. This is a value that has contributed to the various liberation movements we have seen in the culture. But the freedom of the individual to transact makes little sense in the absence of equal opportunity, for example. The notion of the body as one's private property has stood behind the assertion of the legitimacy of a great variety of sexual life-styles, to cite another example. This particular value, however, is not compatible with all forms of social organization. One generally finds it in societies in which the experience of the individual is not constrained by the boundaries implicit in group membership or by the specific roles one might be required to play if one occupies a particular social position. Such societies tend to be highly competitive, innovative, pragmatic, and loosely structured. Adaptability is at a premium, and consequently, friendships tend to be instrumental and easily terminated.

Such a social organization is not unique to developed societies. There are examples of primitive cultures that are organized much the same as the United States and that display similar value systems. Unlike the United States, however, those societies live at a generally low level of organization. They tend to be hunting/gathering societies, living in small bands with extremely fluid membership. When one has an irreconcilable difference with one's neighbor, one simply joins another group. The United States has achieved a society with a high degree of organization at the economic level in the production and delivery of goods and services, but rather little organization at the cultural level, the realm of shared meanings and values. Our vast technological infrastructure (production, marketing, and communication networks) allows for a high degree of individual autonomy, since it reduces the need for interpersonal contact in the process of daily life. We do not need to speak the same language, primarily because we do not need to speak. This style of life consumes enormous amounts of resources and energy as we all seek to create our small autonomous worlds within the confines of our nuclear families. The rising cost of energy alone may produce profound changes, forcing us to concern ourselves with the public world to a greater extent than has been necessary in the recent past.

We have become accustomed to criticism of American materialism, particularly when confronted by our enormous appetite for scarce resources. Yet there is one way in which America may be the least materialistic society in the world. While we consume resources at an astonishing rate, we seem to place little value on what we consume. A society that values the material world should not dispose of its products at such an alarming rate. It should care for, conserve, and refurbish the world, rather than reduce it to "no deposit, no return." Our real love is not material objects, but the act of consumption itself.

We have built ourselves into a disposable world. The perpetual expansion necessary for the survival of our economic system has produced a constant bombardment of seductive advertising designed to stimulate our infantile cravings and to convince us that our resulting wants are actual needs. Yet each new piece of self-esteem purchased in the form of consumer goods perishes like the grass, only sooner. In a sense, to be a consumer is to live in a constant state of anxiety—are we really all we might be, while we lack the latest offering of the marketplace, that something guaranteed to bring us the better life?

This is familiar territory, but it is highly significant for an understanding of the NRPR in the American culture, which seems always to have been a consumer culture. First we consumed the wilderness and its original inhabitants; then we had a good run at the resources of the Third World. One wonders whether, in order to maintain such a high level of consumption, it is necessary to remain rather empty, like a pipe, so that it all can continue to flow through unimpeded. Certainly there is no point in attaching ourselves to transitory things. And since the world has no enduring values in itself, the only relevant reference point becomes the experience of the self as it consumes. Many critics have pointed out that in our society, the process of making things—work—has been reduced to repetitive labor bearing no observable connection to a finished product. But since that product is itself ephemeral in a consumer culture, what difference would it make if there were such an observable connection?

The consumer culture also has had its effect upon American religion, perhaps leading us to give primacy to religious experience as the essence of religion. Speaking to a mixed audience of conservatives and liberals at a conference sponsored by the Ethics and Public Policy Center, William Muehl, professor of practical theology at Yale Divinity School, reflected upon what he took to be one of the saddest failures of American Christianity—the conversion-experience addict. Muehl noted that during a series of revivals, the same people often will come forward repeatedly in order to relive that rush of experience entailed by conversion.[2] It is as if we have produced consumers of the born-again moment, frozen in the hour they first believed. It is rather like being in love with falling in love. The danger here is that religion will become merely another consumer item. Martin Marty sees the danger as especially threatening within the electronic church. The television ministry, Marty properly notes, does not have a congregation, but a clientele. And if the clientele does not get what it wants from "Lamp Unto My Feet," it can tune in "Jack Van Impe Presents" or "The Old-Time Gospel Hour" or any one of the many others that offers a pleasing product.[3] Ronald Knox, in his monumental study *Enthusiasm,* noted the religious problem inherent in experientially oriented religion. Knox wrote, "An inward experience of peace and joy is . . . the assurance which the soul craves. . . . The strength of this personal approach is that it dominates the imagination. . . . Its weakness . . . is an anthropocentric bias, not God's glory but your own salvation preoccupies the mind, with some risk of scruples, and even of despair."[4]

We will have more to say about the problem of making the self the ultimate reference point for meaning and value. At this point we will only note that the dominant NRPR churches traditionally have focused intently upon conversion and the conversion experience and that they too are vulnerable to the possibility of consumer religion. The move of NRPR churches into the public arena brings with it an increasingly urgent need for an answer to the question, Now that we believe, what do we *do*? Martin Marty has suggested that Roman Catholics, with their tradition of

Christian nurture, may have much to offer the NRPR in this area.[5] We should also point out that mainline and liberal churches are every bit as vulnerable to consumeristic experientially oriented religion as is the NRPR, although in different ways. Then there are also the American versions of religions of the East and the tendency to turn psychology into religion, both of which are almost exclusively experience-focused. The phenomenon exists in every segment and every dimension of American culture.

This loss of the public world stands behind much of the first-rate social criticism coming from both the center and the Left. From the center, Daniel Bell, generally acknowledged as one of the leading voices of neoconservatives, points out that America's economic base is organized along different principles from its culture. The economy, according to Bell, is organized to maximize efficiency, to obtain the greatest return at the least cost. To this end it establishes bureaucracy and hierarchy which develop from the need to coordinate highly specialized activities. Value is measured only by utility. Persons become interchangeable objects—things. In contrast, the culture, Bell writes, becomes the arena for "the expression and remaking of the 'self' in order to achieve self-realization and fulfillment." It is concerned with the "enhancement . . . of the self and the 'whole' person."[6]

The individualism or, more extremely, the obsession with the self which Bell sees as the center of the culture has been criticized also from the Left. Christopher Lasch sees it as being little more than a futile attempt to proclaim our basic problem as a great virtue—namely, true human freedom.[7] As the disposable world slips through our fingers, and the social roles which might themselves give a sense of significance evaporate under the tide of individual freedom, little else besides the self remains to be worked on. Our inability to contribute to an enduring common world turns us inward to the only area we can control. The self, after all, seems uniquely ours, the one "thing" we can make, control, and retreat to for security. Thus what Lasch calls the awareness movement offers a culture of authenticity, in which the primary goal of each individual is to become more and more him- or herself. (One wonders what else one could possibly be.) But the self-identity we are called by the radical culture of the last fifteen years or so to achieve is increasingly cut off from those external structures—society, politics, even language itself—which relate us to one another. Genuine "being together" has been thought possible only insofar as we strip ourselves of our social roles and float into some uncharted realm of mystical togetherness. A reminder of this de-worlded view is visible outside one of the local campus ministry centers. There a sign reads, WHAT IF WE WEREN'T TEACHERS AND STUDENTS? WHAT IF WE WERE JUST FRIENDS? The point, however, is that we *are* teachers and students, or clergy and laity, parents and children. To require us to renounce what we are and what we do in order to establish the primary basis of our togetherness would be to impoverish what we can have together.

Since the 1960s, one of the dominant characteristics of liberal religion has been the desire to cast off the "artificialities" of culture and restructure our communities on some deeper or higher basis. Mary Daly's prescription for feminist religion expresses this tendency with startling clarity. (One could change the names and attribute this precept to almost any culturally radical group of the past fifteen years.)

> [The women's revolution] rejects not only the myths of patriarchy but their externalization in ritual.
>   The need for ritual "reminders" itself betrays the precariousness of the shields against anomy which [the] High Priests, both ecclesiastical and civil, wish to erect.
>   Feminist consciousness of being, then, is anti-ritual because it is so deep.[8]

It is perhaps ironic that a leading voice in a political movement should espouse such an antipolitical vision. It is full of hunger for intimacy and despair for the possibility of achieving it in this world. America's flirtations with eastern religions may well be expressions of the same hunger and despair. Here we discovered an ideology which seemed to suggest that the way out of our sense of isolation and alienation was to go farther inward—to increase the isolation. Once one has penetrated deeply enough, the false self—the ego—would dissolve, allowing the true self—the divine reality within each person—to shine forth. Freedom in this context has nothing at all to do with politics, but with a higher state of being . . . or with a deeper consciousness, to return to Mary Daly's language.

There is also a dark side to such endeavors, which has not been lost on the NRPR, but which, thus far, it has been unable to articulate clearly. This is what we shall call the more-human-than-thou syndrome, without apologies for the pejorative language. It is probably best seen in some aspects of humanistic psychology, which, taken as a whole, has been a well-intentioned attempt to avoid stigmatizing people with the label "mentally ill," seeking to enhance their development as full, authentic human beings.

However, if we make "authentic humanness" the goal of the therapeutic process, where do we leave those who fail in therapy or those who do not even avail themselves of its benefits? Are they less than fully human? That clearly would seem to be the implication. One of our local gurus is described by his followers as the most highly evolved person in Gainesville. Presumably the rest of us can attain that higher level of humanness by sitting at his feet. There is often an insidious underground competition loose in the awareness movement, although the movement itself would eschew competition. What is competed for, however, is not a prize or the ephemerality of victory, but humanness itself.

There are many more examples of the bitter fruit born from the wedding of hyperindividualism to a rapidly changing, bureaucratically organized technological base. The dread with which Americans (properly) view old age stems from the absence of any significant role for the elderly in our culture. Since their skills, knowledge, and values have been rendered obsolete, the best we have been offering them is a life of hobbies, an enforced second childhood. Since parents, too, have few skills worth passing on to their children (the world of production being run by innovative and efficiency-valuing bureaucracies), one can only hope that the setting of the family provides a general orientation toward the world and a refuge from impersonality. The responsibility for socialization, the socialization that will give children the tools with which they might actually build a world, is turned over to other institutions. Since all structures and social roles have been assumed to be artificial and dehumanizing, the educational philosophy that is just now passing into eclipse has valued self-expression, feeling, and spontaneity more than disciplined thinking. In general, children have been confused with plants. One only needs to water and fertilize them, and then get out of the way. But while the oak tree is programmed into the acorn, the adult is not programmed into the child. Children do not simply grow, or unfold, into responsible adults; they are molded—in a sense, created—through interaction. They are, after all, children, not seeds.

One of the more insightful critiques of American culture has been produced by John Wikse. Wikse argues that we have produced a culture of idiocy, taking *idiot* in the sense of "the Greek *idiotes,* meaning a private and separate person."[9]

He illustrates the traditional American male version of idiocy with the following autobiographical account.

I was taught the ethos of self-possession through the earliest coherent story I remember, a bed-time tale which my father used to tell me, called "The Saga of Cowboy Jack." This story is both the most personal and intimate biographical fact of my life and my deepest connection to male culture. I relate it here in order to evidence the political psychology of self-possession, the assumptions about the nature of community and authority implicit in my learning to be a man. Here is my reconstruction of the story:

Cowboy Jack is a stranger. He comes from nowhere, without a past, and ever wanders from town to town, riding his white horse, strong and self-reliant. In each town there is chaos, weakness, desperate need, and fear. An incompetent sheriff faces terrorizing bandits whom no one can identify. . . . Gradually Cowboy Jack discovers the root of the corruption and begins, unassisted, to save things. A heroic battle ensues in which the sheriff gets in the way and gets killed, but Cowboy Jack and the decent people emerge victorious. Amidst general joy Cowboy Jack is offered the job of sheriff and the sheriff's daughter (who has fallen irresistibly in love with him). Cowboy Jack lowers his head in deep gratitude, but with sadness for what he must renounce, declares that his journey is still unfinished, that there is still much work to do elsewhere, that he must ride on his way. Leaving the sheriff's daughter in tears, the townspeople wondering what they will do without him, and a friendly dog chasing after him, Cowboy Jack rides off into the sunset.

Each time my father told me this story I cried myself to sleep, sharing with him the understanding that of course it hurts to be a man, inferring many corollaries: Relationships with women, the experience of community, the possibilities of commitment and continuity in a place, genuine respect and gratification, all are separable from a man and his chosen work. Community is a stifling dependence on others, love is a fearful vulnerability (the sheriff's daughter), and if you stay and care and accept authority and connections with others, if you cease to be a stranger to others, then you're done for (the job of sheriff). Rather, do good deeds, live through your self-defined work, depend on no one, and you will be free.[10]

The charm of this story is that it captures the quintessential American hero. It is Daniel Boone, Natty Bumppo, the Lone Ranger, and our next-door neighbor (if not ourselves). To bring the story up to date, it needs only a paragraph describing Cowboy Jack and the sheriff's daughter having sex just before the battle. What Wikse shows, however, is that we have come to idolize madness—the living of life in individual and private realities. Wikse writes that we have located "reliance, dependence, freedom, power and worth within the individual. What for the Greeks could only characterize a city, namely self-governance [also self-sufficiency], comes in the modern West to define the person." Aristotle's original formulation read, "The man who is unable to share in the benefits of political association, or has no need to share, must be either a beast or a God." It seems that, in modern American culture, we have dug ourselves deeper into our basic problems by pretending they are strengths. To cite Wikse again, "Mere human identity is defined by subjectivity or interiority, the experience of being deprived of intimate and enduring relationships with each other is discounted and is transformed into the meaning of freedom."[11] When isolated individualism becomes freedom, when the structures that relate us to one another become denigrated as artificial and oppressive, when society becomes simply "the system," and when private feeling supplants public discourse, we are celebrating autism as health. Our behavior no longer can be valued according to a framework of shared meaning and values, or even according to its consequences in the world. For the culture of idiocy, the only relevant criteria becomes authenticity—do our actions reflect the self, the whole self, and nothing but the self?

The NRPR's display of fear, then, is no mere paranoid delusion, but an attempt to protect itself from the void at the center of the culture. As one renounces the world in the name of inner authenticity, the result is likely to be public chaos, with society held together only by the formal, mathematical organization of the machine. Yet the NRPR's reduction of our options to either authoritarianism or chaos does not offer a real solution. Like the culture in which it is embedded, the NRPR carries the baggage of Protestant individualism, with all its promises and pitfalls. It was perhaps the genius of Protestantism that placed the need for individual choice and commitment on center stage, but it did so at the risk of undercutting the community—the Church—which its own best thinkers held necessary for the preservation of the faith. When the Protestant tendency to remake each individual into a church mixes with a bureaucratically organized technostructure capable of tending to the necessities of everyday survival, those little self-churches can indeed exist and, further, enjoy the illusion of autonomy. But all relationships outside the self, since they are ultimately part of a "lower" order of reality, eventually take on the characteristics of bureaucracy. Friends can be substituted for each other in much the same way that workers can replace each other on an assembly line. The destructive capability of this arrangement is never more visible than in confrontation with the ultimate life crisis, death. America lacks the mourning ritual and the life affirming continuity it provides, for two reasons: First, there is a general absence of roles in the society; second, since all relationships are secondary to the isolated life of the authentic self, loss through death becomes merely an opportunity to read more or to make new friends.[12]

Whether the NRPR has broken out of these cultural traps, it is difficult to say. Its tendencies toward millennialism suggest that at some levels, it holds rather little hope for the world. Worldwide, millennialism tends to be a movement of despair, espoused not so much by the oppressed as by those who have become socially marginal. Confronted by a universe that seems arbitrarily arranged by impersonal powers (big business, secular humanists, etc.) whose behavior one cannot fathom or predict, the millennialist gives up, choosing instead to place his trust in the coming age.

The millennium, however, will be brought about by divine intervention.[13] Thus the experience that produced what first appeared to be a retreat into millennialism is recapitulated in the vision of the new order. Like the old, the new will be established by great uncontrollable forces. But unlike the old, the new, of course, will be established by *good* forces. The relatively powerless and ultimately alienated position of people in these schemes remains the same. Whether in this age or the next, they remain pawns in a much larger game. The rather despairing attitude toward the world evident in NRPR millennialism also appears in its politics. While Jerry Falwell may take issue with this, it seems to us that the NRPR has lost hope for the establishment of a consensus, as shown by its direct move into power politics. The name Moral Majority also can be read "moral *majority,*" meaning simply 50 percent plus one. If the NRPR can capture 50 percent plus one of the vote, it can simply legislate morality and not bother with negotiation and compromise. The combination of a majority, plus power, renders the achievement of a broad consensus unnecessary. But it is an uneasy victory at best, always at the mercy of the tastes of clientele who must pull the proper levers in the voting booth. Ultimately, the NRPR has no criterion of its success other than the/ size of its following. (These kinds of measures of success—size of following, amount of money or goods accumulated, etc.—may be designated by the term *economy of scale.*)

Those churches that have provided the backbone of the NRPR are themselves susceptible to the economy of scale and to the creation of heroes, or special people with whom to identify. Just as there is little against which the leading spokesmen of the NRPR can measure their success beyond size of following, there is little their congregations can hope for, except to see their leaders do well. Because this is a complex matter, including theological orientations as well as sociological factors, some groundwork must be laid.

At first glance it would seem that conservative and Fundamentalist churches have been able to establish vigorous cohesive communities. Their membership has been growing dramatically during the past fifteen years, seemingly in spite of the fact that they demand much from their members in terms of correct belief and behavior. Yet something of the psychology of millennialism also seems to be pervasive. Having found refuge from the arbitrary unpredictable world of modern American society, members of many NRPR churches may have joined a community just as arbitrary and unpredictable as that from which they escaped. There seems to us to be no way members of the Thomas Road Baptist Church can be certain which position on which issue God, through Jerry Falwell, will require of them tomorrow. By and large, Fundamentalist churches have not operated on the basis of a body of general moral principles that can be brought to bear on ethical problems with some sense of predictability. Instead, they have sought to match each individual problem with an appropriate biblical verse, a kind of moral proof-texting. Abortion is wrong because God knew Jeremiah while the prophet was still in the womb; internationalism is wrong because the tower of Babel episode presents a divine endorsement of nationalism; inflation is wrong because the prophet Amos says disapprovingly, "Ye have made the ephah small and the shekel great"; welfare is wrong because Acts says that those who do not work shall not eat; and somewhere in the book of Proverbs lurks a clear endorsement of capitalism. So it goes, particular texts for particular problems, but little in the way of a coherent body of ethical principles.

This was rather poignantly highlighted in the news conference held by Jerry Falwell after the NAE/NRB Congressional breakfast in January 1981. A young man, clearly one of the Evangelical fellowship, asked whether, in the event of another Vietnam-style conflict, there were any principles upon which young men could base their decision about military service. Falwell did not seem to have such principles upon which to draw for a response—probably the question had never come up before—and the best he could manage was the suggestion that our leaders were trustworthy enough not to allow us to become involved in an unjust war. As ethical theory, that will not serve for long. Besides, Falwell himself has made a career of claiming that our leaders are not trustworthy; that, even worse, they have been enormously destructive. To take refuge in blind trust in matters of war and peace is to refuse to deal with difficult issues in all their complexity and ambiguity. We suspect that an answer to the young man's question must await the appearance of military conflict. When the answer comes, it will no doubt be the result of prayerful consideration, and it probably will endorse American military endeavors, but the ethical guidelines upon which it might be based remain a mystery, or perhaps even nonexistent.

To some extent, this example seems to us to illustrate the general structure of independent Fundamentalist churches. They are thoroughly authority-minded, claiming to understand and observe the "inerrant word of the living God." They also seem to be structured in highly authoritarian ways. The minister *is* the church. (This is why the churches remain independent—that is, not affiliated with a denomination.) It is the minister's interpretation that prevails and that is accepted as the clear, obvious meaning of the biblical text. If one assumes that the Bible is infallible, inerrant, and without contradiction, it could hardly be otherwise. Given the fact that other denominations, even Evangelical denominations, view the Bible as an exceedingly complex and difficult body of material, fraught with ambiguities and contradictions; and that academic study of the biblical texts reaches the same conclusion on the basic of rational (but not hostile) analysis, the maintaining of unanimity of belief in an infallible Bible may well require authoritarianism. Doubt must be banished. The danger arises that thought may accompany doubt into exile. Thus the question remains, Are the principal NRPR churches communities in which conversation can be carried on and consensus achieved? Or are they groups of ultimately isolated individuals, having in common primarily their loyalty to the charismatic leader and his presentation of the clear will of God?

It is not surprising that the Protestant groups that comprise much of the NRPR have traditions of "great preaching." Again the economy of scale applies, and thus the rather amazing precision with which these groups recall the numerical dimensions of revivals. Eleven hundred souls saved in a single service; or was it eleven thousand in seven services? Someone will know, for it is the only measure of success. Thus the NRPR, like the rest of the culture, is fascinated with heroes and lives through them. One of the characteristics of liberal culture denounced by Christopher Lasch in *The Culture of Narcissism* was the tendency to overinflate heroes and then to live parasitically off them. Coupled with this, Lasch saw a tendency to overinflate the self—he called it the grandiose self-image. This results not from an overabundance of confidence, but from its opposite, the emptiness and powerlessness of the self.[14] The grandiose self-image substitutes for real accomplishment. In a manner of speaking, it *must* be overblown, since it is made from thin air.

The NRPR version of this cultural phenomenon, at least insofar as we have been exposed to it, is the "Champions for Christ" sermon. It is often directed at young people—for example, the Liberty Baptist College students who are required to attend Thomas Road Church—and it seems ubiquitous. Its message is that "you can do great things with God. You can save America." There is even a good possibility that "you can be President of the United States." Is this simply optimism, or is it self-aggrandizement? In any case, the seeds of the expectation of greatness are being sown, greatness as it appears in the economy of scale—doing big things, moving in powerful circles, turning the nation around. Missing from this view of life is the redemption of the ordinary from insignificance through association with biblical paradigms. It is not the small act of kindness that is the *imitatio Christi,* but the great gesture. Is it our cynicism that leads us to believe that the average graduate of Liberty Baptist College will not achieve much greatness, as it currently is being measured? We think not. Yet what happens to those seeds planted by the "dare to be great" messages? Do they turn inward and bitterly increase a sense of frustration and rage? Are they turned outward and given vicarious satisfaction in the heady accomplishments of the Big Man, as he lives out what others can only dream of? We perceive that the last option is the one currently operating in the NRPR. The Falwells, Robisons, Stanleys, and others of the NRPR serve as emissaries for their congregations, those thousands who can bask vicariously in the fame and adulation accorded their leaders.

The NRPR leaders seem to inhabit a universe significantly different from that of their followers. For the average member of a NRPR congregation, the world is a highly competitive, anxiety-producing place, with rules made and priorities set by the faceless power of corporate and governmental bureaucracies. Outside the confines of the church is a world without group membership and identity, where those without access to power are virtually invited to be victims. The change that occurs when these people enter the world of their churches is dramatic; they become located as members of particular communities. But the agenda of what to believe and do is still imposed from on high, except that the authority now has a face—that of the principal minister. In contrast to this, the NRPR leaders have spiraled out of the confines of group membership and learned to find their way through the various mazes that structure the larger society. More comfortable with that society in general, having found their way into its board rooms and similar centers of power, they are more free to wheel and deal, to compete successfully, and to adopt a relatively pragmatic stance, at least in relation to the outside world.

Observers are bound to ask whether there is conflict among leaders within the NRPR. Philosophically, little room for conflict exists. Should it occur, not many mechanisms for resolving it are at hand. There is, in fact, some conflict—most of it covert, we suspect—but enough has surfaced to gain expression in our conversations with NRPR figures. Any mention of disagreement was off the record, but airing the details is not our point here. It is, instead, to note that such conflict as does occur is likely to remain underground, where it defies resolution, since the epistemology of the NRPR allows little room for disagreement. If the Bible is the infallible, inerrant Word of the living God, pellucid to all who approach it honestly with common sense and sufficient for all our difficulties, how could ministers of the Word differ markedly on central points of the faith or on momentous moral issues? That is simply something that should not happen. The fact that it does occur could be perceived as scandalous, something to be prayed over, but also perhaps something to be ignored, since it does not accord with the preferred definition of reality.

Billy Graham, speaking before the NAE/NRB meeting in January 1981, illustrated the difficulty of in-house criticism. Reflecting on his overidentification with the Nixon White House and the obvious pain and embarrassment that period had caused him, Graham issued a gentle appeal for spreading the gospel and for action—but *social*, rather than political action. While expressing affection for Jerry Falwell, Graham nevertheless felt it necessary to announce, "I am not a member of Moral Majority." What Graham did *not* say—*why* he is not a member—is as significant as what he did say. Whatever his reasons (and they are doubtless complex), therein lies a dark labyrinth of uncharted, perhaps unchartable passageways. When the mechanisms for expressing and resolving conflict are absent, discretion has little choice but to remain silent.

The epistemology of the NRPR emerges rather naturally in impugning the integrity of its opponents and is a task more easily undertaken when the enemy is an external one. Disagreement suggests error on the part of one party (clearly, *both* may be wrong, or partially right, as well) and error is ultimately attributed to a deficiency of faith or character. Since the literal Word of God is directly accessible to common sense and straightforward faith, error is assumed to be a matter of the will. Speaking to the same NAE/NRB audience which Graham addressed, Adrian Rogers, formerly president of the Southern Baptist Convention, argued that those who do not believe in God hold that position as a matter of choice. "The atheist," Rogers charged, "doesn't want to find God for the same reasons a criminal doesn't want to find a policeman." In short, those whose theological positions differed significantly from those of the assembly gathered in the ballroom of the Sheraton Washington suffered from a lack of integrity. Their disbelief was held to be dishonest, a subject for ridicule rather than for serious engagement. It is reminiscent of John Cotton's reply to Roger Williams, one of the spiritual fathers of contemporary Baptists. Williams charged, in *Bloudy Tenent of Persecution,* that he was being persecuted for following the dictates of his conscience. Cotton answered that Williams was being corrected, not for following his conscience, but for disobeying it, since his conscience would, as a matter of course, acknowledge the clear Word of God perfectly understood by Puritan orthodoxy. Cotton thus claimed to know Williams' conscience better than Williams himself did and consequently accused him of a double falsehood—lying to the public and lying to himself. Here is a mind-set that precludes honest disagreement, substituting instead charges of moral perversity. This way of looking at truth does not augur well for a recovery of the public world.

One way to avoid entanglement in the labyrinths of infighting is to direct all invective outward. So far, this has worked well for the NRPR. The moral issues it is concerned about have provided a common enemy tangible enough to reduce significantly the effects of internal conflict. The causes of the elimination of abortion, pornography, secular humanism, and the like have for the most part overwhelmed the internal differences—the NRPR freely admits and affirms this. Yet one must wonder if that is enough; if a movement focused more on what it opposes than on what it positively affirms can form an enduring basis for social/cultural renewal.

A further area in which the NRPR mirrors the culture it rejects has to do with a tendency to prefer "being" to action. The Left's goal has been to become more authentically human, to attain a higher state of being. The counterpart on the Right is the experience of being born again. The NRPR has struggled with this question and probably will continue to do so. Not Christianizing the nation, but returning it to "moral sanity" is the NRPR's highest public priority. Various NRPR spokesmen in differing circumstances have assured the society that their purpose is not the election of born-again candidates to public office. Yet mixed in with these disclaimers one can find numerous instances in which the election of born-again persons is held to be vital to our national well-being and other instances in which prayer and the study of the "word of God" are deemed necessary qualifications for public office. The often quoted "Righteousness exalts a nation but sin is a reproach to any people" from Proverbs also tends in this direction, for it suggests that worldly success is primarily dependent upon internal purity. In more extreme cases, we find assurances that God will intervene on our behalf in the event of a military conflict with Russia, but only if we truly repent. On one occasion we even heard an evangelist tell his listeners that should the U.S.S.R. launch a preemptive strike against a repentant United States, God would prevent the warhead from landing.

The heart of this conflict seems to relate to the core of Christianity itself. It stems from what has been called the Christ-Mysticism of the apostle Paul—the idea that it is possible to live "in Christ" or "in the Spirit" or, alternately, have "Christ live in" one; to live under the Lordship of Christ, rather than under the lordship of sin. The question posed here is one of internal state (being) and its relationship to external activity (action). The tantalizing promise offered is that it is possible, through the grace and power of Christ, to be so transformed as to live a holy life. In the American political system, this aspect of Christianity may clash head on with Thomas Jefferson's conviction that in matters of public policy, all candidates, even those who, in the sincere opinion of the majority, have been approved by God, must present themselves before the court of reason. The NRPR's affirmation of pluralism which accompanies the call for a return to biblical morality indicates an awareness of the problem of relating faith to the public order. The issue is clearly being wrestled with, although it still may be far from resolution. Numerous branches of the larger Evangelical family are keenly aware of the problem and live at a distance from the NRPR. Groups such as the Evangelicals for Social Action and the sponsors of *Sojourners* magazine have much to contribute to the discussion.

The NRPR's lack of mechanisms for resolving conflict, its peculiar entrapment in the economy of scale, and its difficulties with the being/action problem may make it highly susceptible to internal schism. Differing visions on the part of its leaders may fragment it into followers of Paul, Apollos, and Cephas. The proliferation of religious broadcasting through expanding cable and low-power networks will add pressure toward disunion. Success also may produce dropouts, particularly among Roman Catholics, since abortion is the only issue that has attracted them to NRPR ranks.

Some fragmentation may well be desirable, for it might help decrease impersonality and bureaucracy while increasing local participation. Certainly the return of such a large contingent of previously alienated Americans to the public world is a welcome event, despite the difficulties all are encountering. In our estimation, the NRPR is reacting to one of the central problems of American culture—the loss of the world, the loss of that common body of meaning, values, and creations which gives a society the ability to act in concert and yet respect the particularity of its members. When major court decisions in cases involving parental consent for various weighty undertakings by minor children are rendered against the parents on the basis of privacy, the specter of chaos looms perilously large. The family has indeed been reduced to a collection of isolated individuals—atoms with voices, to use Paul Ramsey's apt phrase.[15] But then, as we see it, the same circumstances have dominated virtually every other dimension of American culture. Critics from many sides have warned that the fragility of relationships represented, but not exhausted by the almost 50 percent divorce rate, cannot be healthy. Others, again from many sides, have lamented the decrease in literacy and the resulting absence of a shared body of deep images of the human condition (traditionally supplied in western culture by such works as the Bible, Greek tragedy, Shakespeare), which provides a common pool for cooperative reflection. Still others have noted the connection between pornography and the violence directed against women, which has been increasing over the past several years, suggesting that we need to resist a view of sexuality in which the person is reduced to a sexual organ, as in the visions of the Marquis de Sade. Environmentalists, for years, have been calling us to care for the natural world, urging us to see it as something more than an inexhaustible supply of consumer items. Gerontologists have been drawing our attention to the plight of the elderly who are given no way to contribute significantly to the public order.

The NRPR is thus by no means alone in its sharp criticism of the culture or in its selection of the issues for attention. We have continually returned to what we have called the question of the public world, because that seems to us to be the heart of the matter. The shared values and assumptions; a common public behavioral standard; the sense of national identity and purpose; a broad consensus regarding public policy; and above all, the ability of individuals to cooperate in building the common world—all these are at present painfully absent from both American culture and the NRPR alternative. In this light, the NRPR appears to be a classic example of anthropologist Anthony F. C. Wallace's "revitalization movements."[16]

Historically, these movements have arisen in the context of the disintegration of a society's "mazeway," that internal "map" of the society carried by each individual, which allows the individual to engage in rewarding behavior. This mental map shows how things and people work and the way each individual fits into the larger society, but it can be rendered ineffective by such events as natural disaster, conquest, or rapid social/cultural change. In such cases, following the old mazeway, the old system of behavior and values, ceases to be rewarding and becomes frustrating and anxiety producing. If the "mazeway disintegration" is severe enough, the society may experience a period of "cultural distortion," in which large numbers of people are alienated, confused, and in general at loose ends. Common cultural symptoms at such a point may include despair and passivity, alcohol and drug abuse, disintegration of sexual mores, and violence.

Occasionally within the chaos, a prophetic figure will arise, offering a new revelation, often received in dreams or trance-states, which constitutes a resynthesized mazeway capable of reducing alienation and of guiding behavior into more rewarding directions. Resynthesized mazeways may include calls for the reassertion of some traditions and the elimination of others, or the incorporation of certain external elements (technology, e.g.) and the rejection of others. They often are nativistic—asserting, as they must, the value and integrity of "our" way of life even while making adaptations. Sometimes they also are utopian and millennialistic. The prophet will gather a core of disciples who will assist in the communication of the new mazeway to the outside society. This process may entail a long difficult period of negotiation, compromise, and adaptation, since the society as a whole seldom adopts the new mazeway intact. Assuming that this process takes place successfully (there is never any guarantee that it will), the culture as a whole can be transformed. If the new mazeway fits the conditions under which the society lives—of which there is no guarantee, since, as Wallace notes, some mazeways have been literally suicidal—the society can enter a period of stability.

It seems clear to us that the NRPR has appeared in a period of cultural distortion; that its prophetic leaders have attempted a resynthesis of the American mazeway and proposed a new vision. Since events in the world seldom arrange themselves in the neatly ordered patterns of theoretical models, we should not be surprised to find a number of discrete stages of the model occurring at the same time. Thus the NRPR is simultaneously formulating its mazeway, communicating its current formulations for the purposes of winning converts, and imposing some restructuring on the society through electoral politics and lobbying. To a lesser extent, it is entering into negotiations with other groups in the society. The last process—negotiation, compromise, and adaptation —is naturally the most fascinating and significant. It is something that can take place only in the context of civility—some neutral public order and language that is respected by the various groups in our pluralistic society and that is capable of linking them together and allowing them to communicate with one another.

There seems to us to be great cause for concern here. The NRPR's strident attacks on humanism (whatever that is, really), its dichotomizing of our possibilities into either a Fundamentalistic view of biblical authority on the one hand or chaos on the other, make such a common meeting ground difficult to attain. Similarly, the occasional strident attacks of the secular Left on the NRPR, its suggestions that conservative Christians return to their isolation, the cries of "Christian Ayatollah" serve the same effect. In our opinion, Martin Marty's recent contribution to the discussion, *The Public Church*, correctly identifies one of our central problems as a loss of civility, even a loss of "faith in civility." Under such conditions conversation ends and is replaced by invective, like bombs hurled by one warring tribe against another.

Civility yields to uncivil bumper-sticker warfare, when non-sequiturs posing as premises turn out to be conclusions. "Abortion is Murder." "A woman's body is her own to do with what she wants." "Guns don't kill people, people kill people." "America: Love It or Leave It." "Make Love not War." Above such stickers there is never an invitation to reason. From under and behind them comes a blast of carbon monoxide.[17]

Finally, the overriding question appears to be whether or not there are places and common languages through which we can reason with one another. In many places, people have taken to arming themselves. Some travel great distances to purchase their weapons. They have begun to blaze away at each other at intersections, stop signs, and parking lots—anywhere there is a possibility of conflict. The shape a viable American revitalization might take is still very much in question. Robert Bellah's premise about the third time of crisis for the American civil religion appears increasingly prophetic. How shall a revitalized American civil religion come to terms with similar movements in the rest of the world—the Islamic revolution, for example? And what can the revitalization say, not about our external relations, but our internal relations—the competing claims to stand in the best traditions of the American enterprise? We have no doubt that some new synthesis must emerge. It will need to go beyond the highly self-critical civil religion espoused by Bellah to find an America to celebrate. It also will need to recover the public order in order to allow Americans significant participation in the molding of an enduring world. There is no guarantee of success, only the promise of struggle. And it is most important that the struggle be cooperative and constructive.

CHAPTER 8

Summary and Prospects

The New Religious/Political Right is a significant force within contemporary American society—there is no mistaking that. Its adherents are taking its mandate and its successes very seriously. Those who oppose it or fear it are taking grim note of it and launching campaigns to counter it. In this book, we are endeavoring to take its measure. All three activities reflect the impact the NRPR has made on American life in a very short time.

It is well to repeat here the source of its membership: For the most part, it is assembled from independent Protestant congregations, many of them Baptist—independent, not Southern or American Baptist—principally from the Midwest and the South. No denominations have endorsed it. The mainline Christian traditions have been quick to denounce it, even though some of their more conservative members have supported it. Also, there must be several hundred thousand (at least) politically and morally very conservative Americans, citizens without a strong religious/theological position, who nevertheless lend it their financial and moral support.

We have remarked earlier on the formidability of the conservative Christian ranks who are not in league with the NRPR. Billy Graham is not, Wheaton College and Fuller

Seminary are not, hard-line Fundamentalism is not, the Southern Baptist Convention is not, and neither are such Evangelical radicals as the Evangelicals for Social Action and the *Sojourners* community.

Just as striking is the rejection of the NRPR by classical political conservatives. As time goes on and the NRPR issues are being joined in public discussion, these prominent conservatives are disassociating themselves from it and often attacking it. This impressive list includes such figures as Barry Goldwater, William Buckley, George Will, Robert Dole, Howard Baker, and most southern Democrats who approve of the Reagan administration's economic policies. In fact, the distinguished Senator from Arizona, who lost the race for the Presidency in 1964 because he was perceived as a rabid right-winger, takes a classical conservative position. From this vantage, he minces no words in depreciating the NRPR. The divergence of the NRPR from classical political conservatism is quite sharp and is surely of dramatic importance. In the main, this split is due to the NRPR's philosophical commitment that America is properly a republic, not a democracy.

In viewing NRPR strength, one begins to gain a clear focus on just who does support it. The range is narrow. It is far Right (but not the ultimate in far-Rightness, since such hard-line Fundamentalists as Bob Jones, Lee Roberson, and Carl McIntyre—and softer, but also firm conservatives such as the people of the Churches of Christ—also repudiate political involvement in the manner of true sectarians). We must underscore just how limited its constituency is, when plotted on political and religious spectrums. It really is quite inaccurate and unfair to stereotype "Evangelicals" or "conservatives" (political as well as religious)—or even "Fundamentalists."

This point may be driven home from still another angle: the distinction between the New Religious/Political Right and the electronic church. Falwell, Robison, Stanley, and some others are indeed celebrities of the electronic church, but many whose ministries participate in this orbit are no more than marginally related to the NRPR. The "700 Club" of Pat Robertson, the most sophisticated of the syndicated programs, produced by a technologically wondrous network—the envy of commercial networks, it has been said—disengaged itself from the political arena in October of 1980.

While its political and moral directions shine through and are clearly Right-leaning, this enterprise has chosen to concentrate on spiritual ministries. Not dissimilarly, Jim Bakker and the "PTL Club" pay sporadic attention to political causes—more often when their operation is criticized by a government agency or when a special occasion, such as the Washington for Jesus rally of April 1980, takes place. If anything, "PTL" is more conservative than "700," but both are choosing to devote their television ministries to individuals needing initial and continuing grace from the Lord.

More could be said, but these descriptions suffice to demarcate the NRPR following. To reiterate: Not all Evangelicals (in fact a small minority) line up with the NRPR, nor do all Fundamentalists; most leaders and viewers of the electronic church are not in liaison with the NRPR; classical political conservatives are far more likely to ignore or denounce it than to have anything to do with it. Thus it comprises a rather specific and limited following.

Recently published data point to the inflated membership figures claimed by the electronic church and much repeated by the secular press. The audience of the entire electronic church ministry is not 130 million, as was broadly reported in August 1980. Nor does the correct figure rest close to 100 million, or 60, or 40, or 30, or 25, or 20 million, as variously reported. Both the Nielsen and Arbitron reports place the weekly viewing audience of late 1980 at a figure below 10, but higher than 7 million. This datum is further qualified by other findings: (a) A great deal of multiple program viewing goes on; and (b) the audience appears to be slowly declining. All these facts and figures, it should be remembered, refer to the electronic church generally. According to Nielsen findings, Falwell and the "Old-Time Gospel Hour" ranked fifth on that list in November 1980, with a weekly total audience of 1,440,000; James Robison's ministry was the only other representative from the NRPR in the top ten, amassing 575,000.[1]

These data are sobering in regard to the subject of the movement's size. Massive and rapidly growing it does not appear to be. Its political clout is somewhat out of proportion to its size, as far as we can ascertain. This may mean a couple of things: first, that many who support the cause do not worship by means of the televised religious services; and second, that organizational efficiency may be a more accurate indicator of success than the numbers of the viewing audience.

Efforts to draw a profile of NRPR members and supporters accomplish an auxiliary goal as well: They show that the informal coalition is extremely varied and loosely allied. Beyond any doubt, Moral Majority, Inc., is the core of the movement. Attached to it are some other organized religious causes: Christian Voice, The Roundtable, National Christian Action Coalition, Stanley's IN TOUCH Ministries, James Robison's sphere of influence, and more; largely political-interest groups such as the right-to-life groups, various anti-pornography organizations; and finally that large (as we suspect) contingent of very conservative Americans who own no strong affiliations either religiously or politically, but who share the NRPR's moral/political passions. Perhaps it is not excessive to say that as Jerry Falwell and Moral Majority, Inc., go, so goes the NRPR. It may be that he has reached a similar conclusion and that this has contributed to the increasingly blurred distinction between Moral Majority, Inc., and the "Old-Time Gospel Hour" in his recent direct-mail campaigns. A second figure does loom large, however—namely, Senator Jesse Helms. Around him and his Raleigh, North Carolina-based fund-raising organization, the Congressional Club, a great deal of activity stirs. But the list of celebrities capable of galvanizing public support and of being directly on call to the President and leaders of Congress when key issues are at stake begins to run thin, once you pass Falwell and Helms.

The fading of these two stars from the national center stage—a most unlikely event in the immediate future—would make a difference by depriving the cause of stalwarts who have the power to rally large-scale support. But additional organizations exist and flourish, especially in the interest of affecting state and local elections. Also, that amorphous company of the not-very-religious is large and shows all signs of stability. The NRPR would continue without its most visible and charismatic leadership. But Falwell and Helms perceptibly influence the prosperity of the cause.

The summer 1981 nomination of Sandra D. O'Connor for a seat on the Supreme Court illustrates the powerful place occupied by key individuals. Immediately upon putting her name forward, President Reagan felt obliged to speak directly with Falwell and Helms by way of reassuring and persuading. While hardly a controversial figure, O'Connor had a record of moderate positions on abortion and the Equal Rights Amendment. Reagan had made certain pledges to the Christian Right; he also was determined to retain their support as the honeymoon period wore off. (We suspect that he was also trying to "bring them along" to a more negotiable stance, especially the teachable Falwell.) In any event, the President made a phone call to Lynchburg and invited the senior Senator from North Carolina to the White House. This episode may have been something new in recent American politics—a sitting President sufficiently beholden on limited and extremist political positions to a "televangelist" and one Senator that he could not wait for them to call him. But the President knew what he was doing. Not only was there politics to play; there was also a religious/political "central committee" which symbolized a major force in the society and which had to be addressed as such. Falwell and Helms symbolized more than a cult of personality; they also represented a sizable identifiable constituency, to which, because of political debts and pledges, the President was accountable—another example of the NRPR as a force to be reckoned with.

Ronald Reagan and the NRPR owe each other a great deal. Moreover, their respective futures are co-implicated. This sector of the electorate helped Reagan gain the Presidency. Its surfacing bespoke something of the mood of the country and, at the same time, assisted in crystallizing conservative opinion. One wonders, however, how durable this relationship will be. Already it has been necessary for the President to call them to explain and/or persuade, as we have just seen. Also, for several months he has had to reassure them that their chief moral concerns stand high on *his* list, too; but pressing those concerns must await the strengthening of a depressed and inflated economy and a military defense in perilous condition. To which all politically astute observers can only say, Of course! That's how politics works. But this is precisely an irritant in relations between the NRPR and Reagan, we predict. First, the NRPR is so new at the game that it has acquired little political experience. Second, nonnegotiability is the rhythm of its mentality, a kind of commitment as well as a habit.

Ronald Reagan is already disappointing many in the NRPR. His own positions have moved in a somewhat centrist direction—necessarily so, since he is the President of *all* the people. Perhaps his rapport with the NRPR will prove adequate to guide them into more moderate, generally responsive positions. We can only wait and see. Hadden and Swann *(Prime Time Preachers)* may be quite right in assessing Jerry Falwell as a man doing some growing, doubting, listening, and moderating as his world enlarges. He is far from the bigot, in style or position, that many have inferred him to be. It is possible that his posture will evolve to the what-we-want-is-equal-time philosophy he has been known to enunciate. Some of the responsibility, or promise, as you will, of a modified Falwell doubtless rests in Ronald Reagan's hands. As for the actual outcome, we can only wait and see. It was necessary to the NRPR that Reagan be elected; their spiritual gaskets might have been blown to high heaven, had he not been. It is a possible irony that their success in November of 1980 may lead to the mollification, slight or pronounced, of a hitherto adamant cadre of very convinced conservative Christians.

While projecting and speculating, we must also dare to ask, If failure comes, how will the NRPR react? It is possible, after all—and most likely, judging by the course of political history—that the mood of the country will shift and that the political influence of this movement will wane. The only questions are, When? and, In what directions? Beyond those conditions, any number of scenarios is conceivable: strife or scandal inside the movement; the death of key leaders; the return to power of the Democratic Party; and so forth.

When disappointment comes, what do these devout Christians do? One set of possibilities is despair, bitterness, and retreat to the previous stance of sectarianism. Another alternative is an increased apocalypticism. A third is renewed vigor, heightened dedication, and an even more intense commitment to God's will for them. The last is the most likely. History teaches that the devout go on believing, no matter what, even in the face of "disconfirmation"; even "when prophecy fails." In his book with that title, Leon Festinger has said that "a man with a conviction is a hard man to change." The NRPR inculcates that quality of loyalty. Nevertheless, it is quite possible that a severe loss of political influence or a fairly general discrediting from one or more quarters could produce a retreat from the political sphere. There is not apt to be loss of faith or modification of theological convictions, however.

Decisive retreat from its current political involvement is not predictable, although some smaller nagging problems may be. One key issue (touched on in chapter 5) has to do with the responsibility of candidates who find political action committee (PAC) activities objectionable, but see them as beneficial in election campaigns. Political pragmatism counsels, Accept the support, but avoid close identification. Both Daniel Quayle and James Abdnor are widely reported to have told NCPAC (the National Conservative Political Action Committee headed by John "Terry" Dolan) to get lost, during the 1980 campaign. The committee stayed, however, and its negative advertising clearly injured their opponents, Birch Bayh and George McGovern.

When one considers the fact that Jesse Helms was able to raise $7 million for his senatorial campaign, with 160,000 out of 190,000 contributors residing outside his home state, some possibilities acquire a sharp focus. The injection of vast sums of money into state elections could very well distort those races, decreasing local power and control and even diverting attention away from local concerns. In the late spring of 1981, several leading Republicans withdrew from the advisory board of an anti-abortion group when the organization announced its "hit list" for the 1982 elections. The vast majority of the members of the government who agree with Representative Paul Simon's assessment that "politics admits the possibility of sin" (and hence requires compromise and tolerance) appear to regard PAC activity, single-issue groups, and the NRPR as destructive of the American political process.[2] We should be on the lookout for similar developments in local NRPR groups, and certainly in the interdenominational coalitions which will arise to oppose the NRPR. We have seen some indications that a few local NRPR groups have begun to question the amount of power given to distant PACs which do not share local and regional concerns and are responsible to no one. We can only contemplate with fear a political process dominated by a handful of PACs. Already the first negative advertising of the 1982 campaign has been aired, like the opening salvos of an impending war. The liberals, too, are gearing up their PACs, preparing their hit lists, and producing their negative advertisements. The 1982 campaign promises to degenerate into a totally unedifying spectacle. We can expect a political year with all the depth of a commercial.

Those who have actively involved themselves with the NRPR out of genuine concern for the nation almost certainly will need to deal with these issues. At its best, this movement has rescued some people from the politics of personality so dominant in our culture and has demanded that they take up questions of more substance (never mind the excessively narrow focus). The hope is that the list of issues will broaden and that some issues will move from the realm of declamation to that of discussion. One major gain has been achieved, in that some people have been reoriented from withdrawal from the world to a sense of responsibility for it.

Cynical manipulation by politicians more eager for its votes than for its prayers is a prospect the NRPR realizes it will face. Falwell's continued reliance upon the New Right for collaboration with Moral Majority in its sponsorship of political-action training increases the chances of such manipulation. One bulwark against such tendencies is the autonomy of local MM organizations. However, in our calls to various state MM headquarters around the country, we found that part-time volunteer pastor-directors were being replaced by full-time professional executive directors. It is too early to determine in any detail what this change signifies, but a number of possibilities suggest themselves.

It seems that a kind of second-stage development is taking place, one which may increase efficiency and strengthen the national organization, as well as confirm Falwell's claim that MM is not a religious movement. Yet central organizations often grow stronger at the expense of local interests: Bureaucratization always carries risks—primarily, that the organization will become increasingly distant from local concerns and resistant to local input. Moral Majority could find itself fast becoming just another bureaucracy and losing touch with its constituencies as a result.

Some signs point to the tightening of Falwell's control over MM, with the predictable result that the organization is becoming more closely linked to his personal fortunes. By July of 1981, it had become difficult to distinguish MM from the "Old-Time Gospel Hour." Certainly much of Falwell's OTGH preaching during 1980 and 1981 could have been done just as well from an MM forum.

The OTGH anti-evolution effort entails further overlap with MM. The Lynchburg, Virginia, office of MM is clearly dominant, despite MM's listing of Washington, D.C., as its headquarters. (There have been rumors of a power struggle.) The most recent OTGH fund-raising letters have become virtually indistinguishable from those of MM—a development borne out by the assertion that one can save America by becoming a "faith partner." We suspect that this can be taken as fair evidence that the constituencies of MM and OTGH are substantially the same and that Falwell is attempting to work the same people from both sides of the street. Given Falwell's limited OTGH audience (1.5 million in November 1980, according to the Nielsen survey—not the 25 to 50 million some have estimated), prospects for growth along the path he has chosen also seem quite limited.

We believe that the issue raised here—the extent to which MM is an extension of Jerry Falwell, rather than a less tidy coalition of regional and local communities—is an important one for the future of the NRPR in American society. We are inclined to judge that the more centralized MM becomes, and the less it serves as a public forum on the local level, the less it will have to offer the society. This judgment is based on our conviction that the most significant factor in the ascendancy of the NRPR has been a society-wide loss of people's control over their own fates and an erosion of their sense of competency in action—what we have called loss of the public world. The more MM centralizes, the more its luminaries (particularly Falwell) hand down infallible decrees, and the more local NRPR groups render obedience to marching orders from atop the hierarchy, the more MM will dig its constituency deeper into the pit of powerlessness and alienation, a combination capable of producing rage.

Here the issue of totalitarianism comes to the fore again. This subject has been touched upon before, in taking issue with irresponsible uses of the Holocaust and in using the term *totalitarian* to describe the NRPR's ideological position. Reference to any movement as *totalitarian* amounts to a serious charge; hence some clarification is called for.

We do not mean that the NRPR is a collection of Nazi-like people. The NRPR utopia, after all, features intimate nuclear families, enjoying the benefits of their labors in a recognizably Christian society that allows for freedom of worship. In such a setting, abortion would have been rendered virtually unnecessary by chastity, welfare would have been supplanted by work and Christian charity, and science and technology would flourish, having no trouble respecting the bibilical doctrine of creation. This is very far from the Nazi utopia, which ultimately turned out to be the extermination camp.

By characterizing the NRPR ideology as totalitarian, we mean that we find similarities between the NRPR and the historical manifestations of totalitarianism. Let us recall the specific content of the NRPR's ways of thinking and acting. First, there is its failure to divide its Christianity into "stages" (or phases or realms)—that is, to distinguish between public and private, between what is appropriate in a voluntary organization such as a church, and in an involuntary organization such as a nation. (For virtually everybody, joining another nation just isn't a live option.) Next, the NRPR believes that it knows the Truth, that the Truth is self-evident, and that those who allege that they see other truths do so out of sheer perversity. Consequently, it has been difficult for the NRPR not to impugn the integrity of its opponents—to steer clear of defacing their human dignity. Finally, the NRPR firmly believes it has a divine mandate to impose its "truth" on the society. Or perhaps better stated, the NRPR expects the truth to flow through it into the society. The NRPR is an emissary, a harbinger of the new order (which is also "old-time") and the instrument to bring that new order about. It is the faithful servant to divine authority, submitting itself to God and dutifully obeying orders.

Two particular dimensions of the NRPR phenomenon warrant comparison with totalitarianism: (a) its authoritarianism, especially concerning what can be known as Truth; and (b) its organization of isolated, ultimately atomized individuals into cadres of followers. It is not the *content* (particular goals) of the NRPR that resembles totalitarianism, but its *structure*.

Historically, totalitarianism has attempted to enforce a certain view of reality (often an absurd view) upon its subjects. What is acknowledged as *real,* or *true,* is a matter of definition imposed from above, rather than the result of open questioning, experimentation, and dialogue. Ultimately, the will of the leader, even if that will is far-fetched, inconsistent, or even self-contradictory, determines what is "real." We have learned through both the Soviet and the German experience with totalitarianism that the ability to distinguish truth from falsehood, the real from delusion, can be destroyed, given a sufficiently isolated population and massive indiscriminate applications of force.

It is in the way the NRPR arrives at truth that totalitarian overtones are displayed. Its "truth" is not the result of investigations in the public forum, but is decreed and given the weight of infallibility by its leading luminaries, who, like the leaders of political totalitarianism, claim merely to be following orders from on high. For the NRPR, it is not only religious truth, moral truth, truth about why we are here and what our responsibilities are one to another that can be decreed, but even economic, political, historical, and scientific truth. It is assumed that all, in a sense, are required to see things the way the NRPR does—certainly all are responsible to see things the NRPR way or else be found wanting, at least on the day of judgment. Too frequently, critics of the NRPR have been ridiculed; too infrequently have they been engaged. Too often the integrity of critics has been assaulted and their criticism dismissed as irredeemably tainted by its polluted source. While the NRPR grants its opponents the right to speak, it also confidently asserts a priori that they have nothing to say. The NRPR's tendency to deny others a legitimate place from which to speak is singularly destructive of the foundation upon which a workable democracy (or even a democratic republic) is built.

In its campaign against the teaching of evolution, the NRPR flirts with the legislation of reality. In a strongly worded essay critical of the NRPR which appeared in the *New York Times*, Isaac Asimov reminds us that while it is true that evolution is "only" a theory, so gravity, relativity, and the like are also "only" theories. "Creationism," which the NRPR pushes as of equal scientific validity with evolution, however, is not even a theory—it is not "a detailed explanation of . . . the universe's working . . . based on long observation . . . experiment . . . and careful reasoning from those observations and experiments."[3] In 1948, the leadership of the Soviet Union decreed genetics a false science, on the grounds that it contradicted the "truth" of Marxism/Leninism, and it preferred instead to impose the quackery of Lysenko, with disastrous results for Soviet agriculture. Asimov fears, at worst, an American version of the Lysenko affair, producing "a generation of ignoramuses ill-equipped to run the industry of tomorrow, much less to generate the new advances of the days after tomorrow."[4] While Asimov may have been unduly alarmist, the fear about legislating reality is not misplaced. The NRPR does claim a special status for its program which exempts it from measuring up to the criteria properly required of proposals offered to the public realm.

As historians, we find the NRPR's approved "history" of the United States severely lacking in accuracy, coherence, and even plausibility. It is not that this is merely poor history, but that it is *pathetically* poor history, put forth with a triumphant and vehement confidence that boggles the mind. The NRPR literature presumes to explain everything—and explain it with a few simple "truths." It is the kind of thinking that searches for the magic key that will unlock everything—the clear, simple, master plan that will make it all fall into place. The result is sweeping and simplistic.

This is also Messianic thinking, another characteristic of totalitarianism. There is a deep-seated longing to project all our aspirations onto a hero and to let him do everything for us, in exchange for our unswerving loyalty and obedience. In Jerry Falwell's words:

> Why do we have so few good leaders? . . . What we find missing is the mighty man, that man who is willing . . . to stand up for what is right. We are hard-pressed to find today that man in a governmental position, that man of war, that judge, that prophet, that preacher who is willing to call sin by its right name.[5]

In short, all we lack is the Messiah. It is the NRPR's conviction that he could be at hand that takes us aback. A movement which hungers for that kind of leadership will further undercut its constituents' sense of competence, thereby deepening their helplessness. How are they to distinguish between a Leader and a *Fuehrer*? How can they know whether or not the authoritarianism will be benign? Let us again state our belief that the programmatic content of the NRPR—what it would like to see come about—is not totalitarian. Its totalitarian dimensions show up in its structure—its way of justifying and proclaiming what it "knows" to be "true." It is our concern that the structure of the NRPR could just as easily bear a different content.

The ability to maintain an imposed reality depends upon keeping one's subjects isolated from the outside world (which presents alternate realities) and from one another (which prevents them from checking their perceptions with one another and from expressing their doubts). It is this which strikes us as so significant in the unpredictability of the virtually divine decrees issued in communities such as Falwell's Thomas Road Baptist Church. Although NRPR leaders will claim that the Bible serves as a severe limit upon arbitrary and whimsical pronouncement, it is nevertheless true that the NRPR has no organized system of principles which might render its reading of the Bible predictable and consistent. The authoritative text means whatever the leader says it means, and as Charles Bergstrom of the Lutheran Church in America has pointed out, NRPR readings of the Scriptures are highly idiosyncratic and "liberal."[6] Despite claims to the contrary, the NRPR admits no independent criteria against which the preachments and pronouncements of its leaders can be judged.

The NRPR types of churches that we have seen allow their members little room for such judgments. Pressed in upon one another, often surrounded by the ubiquitous cameras and microphones, NRPR congregations have been reduced to a state of passive obedience. They are told what to believe on a wide range of subjects, denied the privilege of publicly expressed doubt, and given precious little to do, even in worship, beyond attending to and supporting the Big Man.

It is noticeable that in these churches the Bible is not often read—only preached. It is as if a Bible lesson—read without commentary, more or less "hung out there" to work its mysterious effect on the people—would threaten the minister's control over his obedient flock. This recalls an earlier assessment—that the NRPR does not really trust God. Perhaps that is why it tends to be so authoritarian on matters of belief . . . and why conversion sermons are constantly preached to the converted.

The electronic church could easily play a significant role in the future shape and impact of the NRPR. In *The Emerging Order,* Jeremy Rifkin envisions a world in which the NRPR-type Christian never needs to come into contact with the outside world. From the Christian morning news, to the Christian soap opera, to the Christian nightclub, to the Christian "Tonight Show," the electronic media have made possible the living of a hermetically sealed life.[7] In a setting where all one's information comes from a single source, and all one's contacts are with like-minded people, what will happen to one's ability to judge reality? This is an image of isolation—and ultimately, intellectual and spiritual desolation. Perhaps the greatest problem with the electronic church is that it cannot be a church—the Body of Christ—precisely because it is disembodied. William F. Fore's account of the responses he received to a *TV Guide* article on the electronic church is the most startling piece we have seen on this phenomenon. Fore's angry respondents claimed more of a sense of intimacy, community, and personal involvement with television ministries than with their local churches, where they receive "a cold howdy-do and good bye."[8] Imagine! More intimacy in relation to an image on a screen than to flesh-and-blood communities! And yet perhaps this judgment is not surprising. Real communities are inevitably untidy. One is always jostled, challenged, occasionally overlooked as flesh-and-blood congregants vie for the attention of flesh-and-blood clergy who do not smile through cameras, video recorders, satellites, and picture tubes directly into our eyes saying, "You are loved" (whoever you are). Deep within our isolation, are we becoming incapable of tolerating the ambiguities of real communities, preferring instead the counterfeit intimacy of the electronic image? If so, it does not augur well for our collective endeavors.

We have chosen to address these issues and to write strong words because we believe America is facing some severe tests. The particular shape of our society historically has been a breeding ground for totalitarian-type movements (by no means limited to the Right). We reiterate our contention that one of the most pressing tasks facing Americans is the reconstitution of communities—not merely spiritual communities, but communities of the all-too-stubborn flesh—those that attend to the mundane affairs of our common life. The more competently local groups of Americans are able to work out their own destinies, the healthier our society will be. Our churches offer one of the few forums of the people in which that work can be undertaken. We take heart in the allegiance the NRPR swears to the Scriptures of Judaism and Christianity. We fervently hope that the Evangelical community will be able to reach out to the NRPR and deepen its biblical witness, helping it to resonate to biblical idioms, rather than repetitiously appealing to biblical authority. A Jerry Falwell with the social conscience of *Sojourners* would make the demons tremble.

Ironically, the reduction in the scope of government implemented by the Reagan administration may be a step toward traditionally liberal goals. Coalitions of people, liberals and classical conservatives alike, who are dedicated to the preservation of the Republic are beginning to emerge. Leading figures of the mainline and Evangelical traditions are calling for the churches to prepare to fill the vacuum that will be created by reductions in government services. We can only hope that such efforts will be successful, that they will allow increasing numbers of people to participate in and bear responsibility for our common life, and that God will bless those who help one another.

NOTES

Chapter 1. What Is It?

1. Quoted in Marguerite Michaels, "Billy Graham: America Is Not God's Only Kingdom," *Parade* (February 1, 1981).
2. Quoted in "The Concerns and Considerations of Carl F. H. Henry," *Christianity Today* 25 (March 13, 1981):22.

Chapter 2. Where It Fits

1. Franklin Hamlin Littell, *From State Church to Pluralism* (Garden City, N.Y.: Doubleday & Co., 1962).
2. Martin E. Marty, *Righteous Empire* (New York: Dial Press, 1970), ch. 17.
3. George M. Marsden, *Fundamentalism and American Culture* (New York: Oxford University Press, 1980), pp. 3-8, *et passim.*
4. For a profile of Evangelical/Fundamentalist varieties of social ethical positions, see Robert E. Webber, *The Moral Majority: Right or Wrong?* (Westchester, Ill.: Cornerstone Books, 1981), chs. 8, 11.

Chapter 3. Theological Orientation

1. George M. Marsden, *Fundamentalism and American Culture* (New York: Oxford University Press, 1980), p. 3.
2. Reinhold Niebuhr, "The Concept of 'Order of Creation' in Emil Brunner's Social Ethic," *The Theology of Emil Brunner,* ed. Charles W. Kegley (New York: Macmillan Co., 1962), pp. 265-74.
3. *Ibid.,* p. 267.
4. *Ibid.,* p. 266.
5. *Moral Majority Report* 1/5 (May 1, 1980):10.

6. Quoted in Ernest L. Tuveson, *Redeemer Nation* (Chicago: University of Chicago Press, 1968), p. 127.
7. Martha Rountree, testimony at the hearings before the Subcommittee on Courts, Civil Liberties, and the Administration of Justice of the Committee on the Judiciary. House of Representatives, 96th Congress, Second Session on S450, Prayer in Public Schools and Buildings—Federal Court Jurisdiction. No. 63 (Washington, D.C.: U. S. Government Printing Office, 1981), p. 384.
8. Jerry Falwell, *Listen, America!* (Garden City, N.Y.: Doubleday & Co., 1980), p. 98.
9. David Little, paper presented at Ethics and Public Policy Center Conference on Christianity and Politics: Competing Views, April 1981.
10. Thomas Jefferson, cited in Earl Raab, ed., *Religious Conflict in America* (Garden City, N.Y.: Doubleday & Co., 1964), p. 6.

Chapter 4. Organization, Structure, Impact

1. *Moral Majority Report* 1/11 (April 15, 1980).
2. Christian Voice Moral Government Fund (cited hereafter as CVMGF), memorandum (n.d.).
3. Christian Voice, recruiting packet (n.d.).
4. CVMGF, "Christian Right 1980 Election Perspective" (November 1980).
5. CVMGF, press release (October 29, 1980).
6. *Moral Majority Report* 1/3 (March 14, 1980):14.
7. Moral Majority, fund-raising letter (n.d.).
8. *Moral Majority Report* 1/5 (May 1, 1980).
9. *Conservative Digest* 7/1 (January 1981):4-5.
10. *Ibid.*, p. 5.
11. William Chasey, *The Legislative Scenario* (Arlington, Va.: Roundtable Issues and Answers, n.d.).
12. Plymouth Rock Foundation, *Background Briefings and Biblical Principles Concerning Issues of Importance to Godly Christians* (Marlborough, N.H.: Plymouth Rock Foundation, n.d.).

Chapter 5. Reactions

1. Eyewitness account.
2. A Pastoral Letter from the Bishops (October 8, 1980).
3. Peter Berger, "The Class Struggle in American Religion," *Christian Century* 98/6 (February 25, 1981):194.
4. "A Statement on Religion and Politics," Lutheran Council in the USA.
5. Pastoral Letter from Bishops.
6. Berger, "Class Struggle," p. 197.
7. Peter H. Davids, "God and Caesar," pt. 2, *Sojourners* 10/5 (May 1981):27.
8. Robert Zwier and Richard Smith, "Christian Politics and the New Right," *Christian Century* 97/30 (October 8, 1980):939.
9. Editorial, *Christianity Today* (September 19, 1980).
10. Charles Bergstrom, "When the Self-Righteous Rule, Watch Out!" *Focus on Governmental Affairs* (Lutheran Council in the USA) 13/12 (December 1979).
11. Berger, "Class Struggle," p. 194.

12. Carl F. H. Henry, "Interview With," *Christianity Today* 25/5 (March 13, 1981):21, 22.
13. *Ibid.,* p. 23.
14. Editorial, *Christianity Today* (September 19, 1980).
15. Henry, "Interview With," p. 23.
16. Bishop Paul Moore, Jr., address to the 203rd Annual Convention of the Diocese of New York, September 30, 1980.
17. Keith I. Pohl, "What Is Right and Wrong with the 'New Religious Right': A Critical Analysis," *Engage/Social Action Forum* 67 (January 1981):33.
18. Davids, "God and Caesar," pt. 1, *Sojourners* 10/4 (April 1981):15.
19. Editorial, *Christianity Today* (September 19, 1981).
20. Paul D. Simmons, "Fundamentalism: Courting Civil Religion," *Report from the Capital* (Baptist Joint Committee on Public Affairs) (June 1981):4, 5.
21. *Ibid.,* pp. 5-6
22. "Statement on Religion and Politics," Lutheran Council in the USA.
23. Bergstrom, "Old Strident Sounds from the 'New Right,'" *Engage/Social Action Forum* 67 (January 1981):23.
24. Simmons, "Fundamentalism," p. 4.
25. Berger, "Class Struggle," p. 196.
26. Henry, "Interview With," p. 23.
27. Allen J. Lichtman, "The New Prohibitionism," *Christian Century* 97/33 (October 29, 1980):1029.
28. Editorial, *Christianity Today* (September 19, 1980).
29. Walter E. Fauntroy, Member of Congress, press release (October 16, 1980).
30. Martin E. Marty, *The Public Church* (New York: Crossroads Books, Seabury Press, 1981), pp. 143-44.
31. Milton Ellerin and Alisa Kesten, "The New Right," *Trends Analysis Report* (American Jewish Committee) (November 18, 1980):9.
32. Alexander Schindler, "Report of the President of the Union of American Hebrew Congregations to the Board of Trustees" (November 21, 1980).
33. *Ibid.*
34. Marc Tanenbaum, "Could Be . . . ," *Hadassah* (April 1981):48.
35. *Ibid.,* pp. 48, 50.
36. Arthur Hertzberg, "Can't Be . . . ," *Hadassah* (April 1981):21, 47.
37. Jerry Falwell, *Listen, America!* (Garden City, N.Y.: Doubleday & Co., 1980), p. 113.

Chapter 6. Civil Religion

1. Will Herberg, "America's Civil Religion: What It Is and Whence It Comes," *American Civil Religion,* ed. Russell E. Richey and Donald G. Jones (New York: Harper & Row, 1974), p. 78.
2. Sidney E. Mead, "The 'Nation with the Soul of a Church,'" *American Civil Religion,* ed. Richey and Jones, pp. 52-53, 60-61.
3. Clifford Geertz, *The Interpretation of Cultures* (New York: Basic Books, 1973), p. 90. Geertz uses the phrase "general order of existence" in a rather famous (or infamous) definition of religion which is an essay in itself. In short, Geertz argues that religions project (or acknowledge) an ultimate scheme of things (general order of existence) which they give life to, celebrate, and

reinforce in religious activity (ritual) so that persons are disposed to feel, think, and act as if the religion were true.

4. Robert N. Bellah, "Civil Religion in America," *American Civil Religion,* ed. Richey and Jones, p. 33.

5. Robert N. Bellah and Phillip E. Hammond, *Varieties of Civil Religion* (San Francisco: Harper & Row, 1980), ch. 5, "The Rudimentary Forms of Civil Religion."

6. Jerry Falwell, *Listen America!* (Garden City, N.Y.: Doubleday & Co., 1980), p. 244.

7. Charles F. Stanley, *Stand Up, America!* (Atlanta: IN TOUCH Ministries, 1980), p. 48.

8. Falwell, *Listen, America!* p. 106.

9. Tim LaHaye, *The Battle for the Mind* (Old Tappan, N.J.: Fleming H. Revell Co., 1980), p. 100.

10. Stanley, *Stand Up, America!* p. 6.

11. Falwell, *Listen, America!* p. 29.

12. *Ibid.,* p. 20.

13. Donald R. Howard, *Rebirth of Our Nation* (Lewisville, Tex.: Accelerated Christian Education, 1979), p. 110.

14. Martin E. Marty, *The Public Church* (New York: Crossroad Books, Seabury Press, 1981), pp. 101-2.

15. Howard, *Rebirth of Nation,* p. 20.

16. Jesse Helms, *When Free Men Shall Stand* (Grand Rapids, Mich.: Zondervan Corp., 1976), p. 15.

17. Joshua Scottow, *Old Men's Tears* (Boston: n.p., 1691), p. 4.

18. Falwell, *Listen, America!* p. 50.

19. *Ibid.,* p. 30.

20. Howard, *Rebirth of Nation,* p. 107.

21. Falwell, *Listen, America!* p. 13.

Chapter 7. Why Now?

1. Donald R. Howard, *Rebirth of Our Nation* (Lewisville, Tex.: Accelerated Christian Education, 1979), p. 246.

2. William Muehl, address to Ethics and Public Policy Center Conference on Christianity and Politics: Competing Views, April 1981.

3. Martin E. Marty, *The Public Church* (New York: Crossroads Books, Seabury Press, 1981), p. 48.

4. Ronald A. Knox, *Enthusiasm, A Chapter in the History of Religion* (Oxford: Clarendon Press, 1950), pp. 2-3.

5. Marty, *Public Church,* p. 35.

6. Daniel Bell, *The Cultural Contradictions of Capitalism* (New York: Basic Books, 1976), pp. 10-14.

7. Christopher Lasch, *The Culture of Narcissism* (New York: W. W. Norton, 1978), p. 27.

8. Mary Daly, *Beyond God the Father* (Boston: Beacon Press, 1973), pp. 143-45.

9. John Wikse, *About Possession: The Self as Private Property* (University Park: Pennsylvania State University Press, 1977), p. 1.

10. *Ibid.,* pp. 11-12.

11. *Ibid.,* pp. 34, 44.
12. Peter Marris, *Loss and Change* (Garden City, N.Y.: Doubleday & Co., 1975), pp. 95-97.
13. It is significant that the NRPR displays a preference for premillennialism—Christ's return before the reign of righteousness—thus emphasizing the discontinuity between the millennium and the present age.
14. Lasch, *Culture of Narcissism,* p. 36.
15. Paul Ramsey, remarks to Conference on Christianity and Politics.
16. Anthony F. C. Wallace, "Revitalization Movements," *American Anthropologist* 58/2 (1956):265-81.
17. Marty, *Public Church,* pp. 110, 132.

Chapter 8. Summary

1. See William Martin, "The Birth of a Media Myth," *The Atlantic* 247/6 (June 1981):7-16; also Jeffrey K. Hadden and Charles E. Swann, *Prime Time Preachers* (Reading, Mass.: Addison-Wesley Publishing Co., 1981), ch. 3, esp. pp. 51, 55.
2. Paul Simon, interviewed by Dennis E. Owen.
3. *New York Times Magazine* (Spring 1981):94.
4. *Ibid.,* p. 100.
5. Jerry Falwell, *Listen, America!* (Garden City, N.Y.: Doubleday & Co., 1980), p. 16.
6. Charles Bergstrom, "When the Self-Righteous Rule, Watch Out," *Focus on Governmental Affairs* (Lutheran Council in the USA) 13/12 (December 1979).
7. Jeremy Rifkin and Ted Howard, *The Emerging Order* (New York: Putnam, 1979), ch. 5.
8. William F. Fore, "Beyond the Electronic Church," *The Christian Century* 98/1 (January 7-14, 1981):29-30.